SHIFT YOUR NARRATIVE

Transform Your Mind, Will, & Emotions

Dr. C. White~Elliott, Ph.D.

Dr. C. White-Elliott, Ph.D.

SHIFT YOUR NARRATIVE

Transform Your Mind, Will & Emotions

clfpublishing.org
909.315.3161

Cover design by Senir Design. Contact info: info@senirdesign.com

ISBN #978-1-945102-93-6

Printed in the United States of America.

Dedication

To all who can envision a better tomorrow
and understand it will manifest when
changes are made today.

Acknowledgment

Jesus the Christ, my Lord and my Savior,
the one who gave me the gift to write
and express love, care, and concern
for all readers.

Contents

INTRODUCTION

It is important to note that a person's life does not necessarily have to be completely in shambles for mindful transformation to be necessary. Just one area of his/her life can require immediate attention. And, when that realization comes about, he/she should immediately attend to committing to transforming in order to prevent other areas of his/her life from becoming contaminated as well.

So, who was this book written for? It was written for the conscientious individual who is willing to take a look at his/her life to perform an honest examination of where he/she is currently positioned and will bravely compare it to where he/she desires to be. Then, after doing so, he/she will begin to navigate through the transformation, knowing the process may be difficult but not impossible. Personal transformation is achievable.

Looking at Dr. Martin Luther King, Jr.'s "What is Your Life's Blueprint?" speech, he provided insightful information about how we should view our life as we exist within this earth realm.

In answering his own question that he wanted his audience to ponder, he provided two components of the blueprint to start them on the right train of thought. According to King, one's life blueprint is designed to serve "as the pattern" (King) for his/her life. It includes

1. "a deep belief in your own dignity, your worth, and your own somebodiness" (King), and
2. "the basic principle of determination to achieve excellence in your various fields of endeavor" (King).

As you read through the pages of this book, have a highlighter and a pen in hand, so you can make notes and highlight important information along the way. Keep your mind open to the information you will read and take time to ponder on it, allowing it to seep in.

Welcome to the journey of your life's transformation!

PART I

Your Past & Your Present

CHAPTER ONE

The Human Design

Chapter One
The Human Design

"And God said, 'Let us make man in our image, after our likeness: and let them have dominion over the fish of the sea, and over the fowl of the air, and over the cattle, and over all the earth, and over every creeping thing that creepeth upon the earth'."

Genesis 1:26 (KJV)

In order for us to get to the heart of the matter about how to transform our personal life journey (our narrative) from its current condition to one that is increasingly fruitful and more peaceful, we must first examine the creation of mankind. When God created humans, He employed a special design and had a specific function for them. Without understanding our unique design, behavior patterns, and thought patterns, it will be difficult to conceptualize our current condition in comparison to one that exemplifies our Creator and His original intent for our lives. Furthermore, this information will assist us in understanding why one would desire a shift from his/her current life to another one. Possessing the knowledge and understanding will place us in a position where we can choose the status quo or opt for a lifestyle more befitting a child of God's Kingdom. In laying out this information in detail, we will be equipped to begin our transformation while releasing the mindset of conformity (one we may not even know we currently possess, because of course, we would never claim to being a conformist of a mediocre or substandard life or think we fit the definition.)

To understand our unique design, we must go to the Word of God. The book of Genesis (the book of beginnings) shares the account of man's creation. Genesis 1:26 (KJV) says, *"And God said, Let us make man in our image, after our likeness: and let them have dominion over the fish of the sea, and over the fowl of the air, and over the cattle, and over all the earth, and over every creeping thing that creepeth upon the earth."* Notice the words, *"after our likeness."* These words refer to many conditions in which man was created in the image of God. However, the primary condition being referred to is the "spirit" condition. God is a spirit; therefore, man is a spirit. Keep this in mind. We will deal with this in a moment when we discuss the components of which humans are comprised.

Genesis 1:27 (KJV) says, *"So God created man in his own image, in the image of God created he him; male and female created he them."* Let's move on to Genesis Chapter Two to learn the intricate details of the process of creation. Verse Seven of Chapter Two (KJV) says, *"And the LORD God formed man of the dust of the ground, and breathed into his nostrils the breath of life; and man became a living soul."* Notice when God created man from the dust of the ground, there was no life in him. He was just a shell; there was no breath, no feelings, no emotions, no movement or actions, no thought processes, no conformity, no ideologies – nothing.

It was not until God breathed the breath of life into the nostrils of man, then and only then did man come alive. When the earthen body received the breath of life (spirit) that God had breathed into him, it was at that moment that man became a living soul. However, even though he became a living soul, it took time before he would find himself in a position where he would be impacted by the world around him and have a need for change within the inner most part of him.

From the details of man's creation, notice the three parts of man: body, soul, and spirit. First, the body was created from the dust of the ground. Then, God breathed into man's nostrils, depositing the spirit into the body. Upon the spirit's entrance into the body, the soul was created, connecting the body and the spirit together. This may be where the term 'soul tie' originated, demonstrating the strength of the soul to connect the body and spirit together. Today though, the term 'soul tie' is used to refer to the souls of two individuals being tied together to create a strong bond between them.

From that detailed revelation, man, therefore, is understood to be a tripart being, and each portion of man has a specific function. The body is the "world-consciousness," connecting to the world around him. The spirit is "God-consciousness," connecting to God, the Father, the Son, and Holy Spirit. The soul is "self-consciousness," finding his very own connection to the world and God through his emotions, will, and intellect.

According to Watchman Nee, "When the spirit caused the body to come alive, man became a living soul, a living person with his own consciousness. A complete person is a tripartite being, a person with a spirit, a soul, and a body. The three elements of [man's] being were fully in harmony one with another. These three were mingled together. According to [Genesis 2:7], man was created with two independent materials- spirit and body. When the spirit entered the body, the soul was produced. The soul is the result of the union of the spirit and the body. The body was dead, but when it met the spirit of life, a third entity was produced, the soul. Without the spirit, the body is dead. When the spirit came, the body became alive. When the spirit is in the body, something organic is produced. This something that is organic is called the soul."

Nee continues with further details to elucidate the purpose of the soul: "The soul serve[s] as the linking chain, the seat of man's personality, making it possible for man to exist [as an independent thinker]. God characterizes man by his soul because in His creation, man's characteristics lie in his soul. The soul represents the man and expresses the characteristics of his personality. The soul is the organ of man's free will, and both the spirit and the body are incorporated into it. It has a free will. If it chooses to obey God, it can make the spirit the master of everything, according to God's design. But it can also suppress the spirit. The spirit is the motivating force behind the soul, while the body is the means to express the soul."

Nee further postulates, "Among the three elements of man, the spirit is joined to God and is the highest. The body is in contact with the material world and is the lowest. In between the two is the soul. It takes as its nature the nature of the other two. As such it becomes the linkage of the other two parts. Through the soul the two parts can fellowship with each other and can work together. The function of the soul is to maintain the spirit and the body in their proper order so that they will not lose their proper relationship with one another. In this way, the body, which is the lowest, will submit to the spirit, and the spirit, which is the highest, will be able to control the body through the soul. The soul is indeed the chief element in man." Nee's statement is presented here to reiterate the points I made earlier in an effort to emphasize the intricate design of man.

As previously mentioned, each part of man (body, soul, and spirit) has a specific function. Let's delve a bit deeper into each part and its abilities and capabilities. As we survey each component, be mindful that "the Bible never tells us that a fleshly person has any life apart from the soul. Man's life is the soul that has permeated the body. When the soul is joined to the body, the soul becomes man's life, for life is but an expression of the soul. Since our present physical life is the life of the soul, the Bible calls our present body 'a soulish body' (I Corinthians 15:44)" (Nee).

The ability to function within the earth realm is permitted via the first component of man: the physical ***body***, which is comprised of bones, organs, a nervous system (nerves and the brain), and the cells that comprise the fatty tissue and epidermis (skin). The body is the visible, physical, external component of humans that provides the ability to interact with the physical world in which it exists via five physical/natural senses: sight, smell, hearing, taste, and touch. The body is the outer shell of the soul.

"Touch consists of several distinct sensations communicated to the brain through specialized neurons in the skin. Pressure, temperature, light touch, vibration, pain and other sensations are all part of the touch sense and are all attributed to different receptors in the skin" (Harvey & Bradford, 2022).

The sense of sight (also known as vision) is created by the brain and a pair of sensory organs - the eyes. Vision is often thought of as the strongest of the senses. That is because humans tend to rely more on sight, rather than hearing or smell, for information about their environment" (Ask the Scientists, 2022).

Hearing "works via the complex labyrinth that is the human ear. Sound is funneled through the external ear and piped into the external auditory canal. Then, sound waves reach the tympanic membrane, or eardrum. This is a thin sheet of connective tissue that vibrates when sound waves strike it" (Ask the Scientists, 2022).

According to Merriam-Webster, "taste is the special sense that perceives and distinguishes the sweet, sour, bitter, or salty, or umami quality of a dissolved substance and is mediated by taste buds on the tongue." According to Merriam-Webster, "the sense of smell is to perceive the odor or scent of [something] through stimuli affecting the olfactory nerves: get the odor or scent of [something] with the nose."

The second component of man is ***spirit.*** This component interacts with God and the spiritual realm via its own set of six senses (five of which correlate to the natural senses): sight, smell, hearing, taste, touch, and faith. It is our spirit that gives us meaning and purpose in life and enables us to love one another, ourselves, and God. Our spirit also gives us intuition between right and wrong.

The spiritual sense of *sight* draws a believer to grow in the ability to see life from an eternal perspective and to evaluate experiences according to God's purposes and priorities, to see from God's point of view. "The sense of *smell* is a more intimate sense than most other senses, for in smelling, the thing that we smell becomes almost a part of us. In detecting a smell, we absorb the essence of it. The fragrance clings to us. The knowledge of Jesus is a fragrance that clings to us. It is the knowledge of Him that is the fragrance! We can smell the purity of Jesus. We can smell His presence. Holiness has a fragrance" (G1 Fourways). The Word says God smells our fragrance, and He spreads it, allowing the beautiful fragrance of the knowledge of His Son to permeate into the hearts of others.

Spiritual listening is your ability to listen deeply, to hear with the ears of your heart. It is a deep hearing of God's voice. In Mark Chapter 4, we read about Jesus teaching a large group of people using parables. When He had finished speaking, He said to them, *"He who has ears to hear let him hear"* (ESV).

"The word '*taste*' comes from the Hebrew word ta'am, which means to savour, to experience" (G1 Fourways). Think of some words to describe taste – delicious, appetizing, sweet, yummy, and divine. Yet, how often do we use words like these to describe our experience of God or the Word of God? I appreciate the fact that David uses the word 'taste' here when referring to the way God comes to us: Psalm 34:8 (ESV) says, *"Oh, taste and see that the Lord is good."* When we taste something, we take it into us, and it becomes part of us. We can see, touch or hear something without it necessarily becoming a part of us. However, when we taste something, it becomes part of us. We transform it into our own being and our own flesh.

In the same way, we taste the Lord (through His Word) and take Him as nourishment and food into our spirit. Thereby, our spirits are transformed. Jesus becomes part of our being. His Word is our food, and this food grows our spirit man and bears fruit within us and is then manifested without and displayed in the lives of those with whom we come in contact. This is the way God wants to come into our lives. He does not want to remain on the outside as something external. He wants to become an intimate part of our being. And this He does through His Word.

The *touch* of God in the heart is an awesome thing. It is awesome because the heart is so precious to us - so deep and intimate and personal. When the heart is touched, we are deeply touched. When the heart is touched, the core of our being is touched. When the heart is touched, someone has gotten through all the layers to the center. It is a real connection. We have been known. We have been seen. We have been pierced. The touch of God is an awesome thing because God is God. Just think of what is being said here! God touched them. Not a husband. Not a child. Not a parent. Not a counsellor. But God. The One with infinite power in the universe. The One with infinite authority, wisdom and infinite love and goodness. That One touched their hearts. How deeply profound and meaningful to be touched by God!

Romans 5:5 says, *"God's love has been poured into our hearts through the Holy Spirit that has been given to us."* God touches our hearts through His Holy Spirit. As Holy Spirit fills us, He fills us with God's love, He touches us deeply within our hearts causing us to experience His presence. He is personal and intimate, and as He touches us, He kindles within us a longing for Him and for His presence. Therefore, after His touch, we begin to seek after Him.

Faith is the sixth spiritual sense. "Faith is a gift from God. *'God hath dealt to every man the measure of faith'* (Romans 12:3). *'But without faith, it is impossible to please him: for he that cometh to God must believe that he is, and that he is a rewarder of them that diligently seek him'* (Hebrews 11:6). If you do not possess His divine faith, you are not pleasing God. Jesus is the author of your faith; He wrote it in His own blood, and the Bible declares that the just will live by it. *'Looking unto Jesus the author and finisher of our faith'* (Hebrews 12:2). Not only is He the author of your faith, He is the finisher of it; there is nothing to be added to it. Jesus made our faith a finished work" (Angley, 1999).

The third component of man is the ***soul,*** which gives us our personality (the animating principle of humans), and through it, we live out our relationship with God and others. The soul is responsible for our thoughts, imagination, judgments, memory, feelings, reason, stimulations, and emotions. It serves as the command center for the person. Neither the body nor the spirit can function in isolation. The soul directs both the body and the spirit, as it serves as "a medium between our spirit and our body, possessing self-consciousness, that we may have our personality" (Bibles for America, 2022). The soul is the outer shell of the spirit.

Of the three parts that comprise man: spirit, soul, and body, our focus is on the soul, as it is the soul that dictates man's narrative. Similar to the composition of man, the soul is comprised of three components: the mind, the will, and the emotions. Within man's soul exists his ability to shape the state of his existence in the earth realm, for it is where his consciousness lies. "Our mind has a conscious part and a subconscious part. The conscious mind is where we do our thinking and reasoning. The subconscious mind is where we hold our deep beliefs and our attitudes. It is also where we have our feeling, our emotion, and retain our memories. Our will is what gives us the ability to make choices. Through a very complex way, our mind, our will, and our emotions are connected to the body through our endocrine, nervous and immune systems" (Faith and Health Connection, 2022).

The Bible gives ample evidence that the mind, will, and emotions comprise the soul in the following categorized verses. These verses demonstrate that man's intellect, mind, ideals, love, stimulations, judgment, will, etc. are all parts of the soul.

THE MIND

The mind is the thinking organ; it is our intellect. Our intelligence, knowledge, and everything that has to do with our mental capacity comes from the mind. Without the mind, man would be totally foolish.

> ***"For wisdom will enter your heart, and knowledge will be pleasant to your soul."***
> **Proverbs 2:10 (NIV)**

****

> ***"Know also that wisdom is like honey for you: If you find it, there is a future hope for you, and your hope will not be cut off."***
> **Proverbs 24:14 (NIV)**

****

> ***"Desire without knowledge is not good—how much more will hasty feet miss the way!"***
> **Proverbs 19:2 (NIV)**

"My son, do not let wisdom and understanding out of your sight, preserve sound judgment and discretion; they will be life for you, an ornament to grace your neck."

Proverbs 3:21-22 (NIV)

****

"I praise you because I am fearfully and wonderfully made; your works are wonderful, I know that full well."

Psalm 139:14 (NIV)

****

"In your relationships with one another, have the same mindset as Christ Jesus."

Philippians 2:5 (NIV)

****

"How long must I wrestle with my thoughts and day after day have sorrow in my heart? How long will my enemy triumph over me?"

Psalm 13:2 (NIV)

****

"I well remember them, and my soul is downcast within me."

Lamentations 3:20 (NIV)

****

"And the peace of God, which transcends all understanding, will guard your hearts and your minds in Christ Jesus."

Philippians 4:7 (NIV)

****

"Who has known the mind of the Lord so as to instruct him?" But we have the mind of Christ."

I Corinthians 2:16 (NIV)

****

"Do not conform to the pattern of this world, but be transformed by the renewing of your mind. Then you will be able to test and approve what God's will is—his good, pleasing and perfect will."

Romans 12:2 (NIV)

****

"One person considers one day more sacred than another; another considers every day alike. Each of them should be fully convinced in their own mind."

Romans 14:5 (NIV)

****

"This is the covenant I will establish with the people of Israel after that time, declares the Lord. I will put my laws in their minds and write them on their hearts. I will be their God, and they will be my people."

Hebrews 8:10 (NIV)

****

"You will keep in perfect peace those whose minds are steadfast, because they trust in you."

Isaiah 26:3 (NIV)

****

"Therefore, with minds that are alert and fully sober, set your hope on the grace to be brought to you when Jesus Christ is revealed at his coming."

I Peter 1:13 (NIV)

****

"The LORD saw how great the wickedness of the human race had become on the earth, and that every inclination of the thoughts of the human heart was only evil all the time."

Genesis 6:5 (NIV)

****

The Will

The will is the deliberating organ, where the power of judgment lies. It makes decisions on whether or not one will do something and whether or not one wants something. Without the will, man would be a machine, following orders and commands rather than being a free-will being as God created him.

"So that I prefer strangling and death, rather than this body of mine."

Job 7:15 (NIV)

****

"If you declare with your mouth, 'Jesus is Lord,' and believe in your heart that God raised him from the dead, you will be saved."

Romans 10:9 (NIV)

****

"It does not, therefore, depend on human desire or effort, but on God's mercy."

Romans 9:16 (NIV)

"I refuse to touch it; such food makes me ill."

Job 6:7 (NIV)

****

"If you are not pleased with her, let her go wherever she wishes. You must not sell her or treat her as a slave, since you have dishonored her."

Deuteronomy 21:14 (NIV)

****

"So I stretched out my hand against you and reduced your territory; I gave you over to the greed of your enemies, the daughters of the Philistines, who were shocked by your lewd conduct."

Ezekiel 16:27 (NIV)

****

"The LORD protects and preserves them-they are counted among the blessed in the land - he does not give them over to the desire of their foes."

Psalm 41:2 (NIV)

"Now devote your heart and soul to seeking the LORD your God. Begin to build the sanctuary of the LORD God, so that you may bring the ark of the covenant of the LORD and the sacred articles belonging to God into the temple that will be built for the Name of the LORD."

I Chronicles 22:19 (NIV)

****

"When a man makes a vow to the LORD or takes an oath to obligate himself by a pledge, he must not break his word but must do everything he said."

Numbers 30:2 (NIV)

****

"The mind governed by the flesh is hostile to God; it does not submit to God's law, nor can it do so."

Romans 8:7 (NIV)

****

"Therefore, just as sin entered the world through one man, and death through

sin, and in this way death came to all people, because all sinned."

Romans 5:12 (NIV)

****

"You see, at just the right time, when we were still powerless, Christ died for the ungodly."

Romans 5:6 (NIV)

****

"Children born not of natural descent, nor of human decision or a husband's will, but born of God."

John 1:13 (NIV)

****

"The person without the Spirit does not accept the things that come from the Spirit of God but considers them foolishness, and cannot understand them because they are discerned only through the Spirit."

I Corinthians 2:14 (NIV)

****

"All of us also lived among them at one time, gratifying the cravings of our flesh and following its desires and thoughts. Like the rest, we were by nature deserving of wrath."

Ephesians 2:3 (NIV)

****

The Emotions

The emotion is the organ of love, hatred, and sentiments. We can love, hate, feel joy, anger, sorrow, and happiness through our emotion. Without the emotion, humans would be void of feelings like inanimate objects, such as wood and stone, making them equivalent to robots, doing things only by command rather than from the desires that emanate from within.

> ***"Tell me, you whom I love, where you graze your flock and where you rest your sheep at midday. Why should I be like a veiled woman beside the flocks of your friends?"***
>
> **Song of Songs 1:7 (NIV)**

****

> ***"Use the silver to buy whatever you like: cattle, sheep, wine or other fermented drink, or anything you wish. Then you and your household shall eat there in the presence of the Lord your God and rejoice."***
>
> **Deuteronomy 14:26 (NIV)**

"Then they got rid of the foreign gods among them and served the LORD. And he could bear Israel's misery no longer."

Judges 10:16 (NIV)

****

"Have I not wept for those in trouble? Has not my soul grieved for the poor?"

Job 30:25 (NIV)

****

"As the deer pants for streams of water, so my soul pants for you, my God."

Psalm 42:1 (NIV)

****

"David was greatly distressed because the men were talking of stoning him; each one was bitter in spirit because of his sons and daughters. But David found strength in the LORD his God."

I Samuel 30:6 (NIV)

****

"On that day David had said, 'Anyone who conquers the Jebusites will have to use the water shaft to reach those "lame and blind" who are David's enemies.' That is why they say, 'The "blind and lame" will not enter the palace'."

II Samuel 5:8 (NIV)

****

"Bring joy to your servant, Lord, for I put my trust in you."

Psalm 86:4 (NIV)

****

"You will never come back to the land you long to return to."

Jeremiah 22:27 (NIV)

****

"No longer will I make you hear the taunts of the nations, and no longer will you suffer the scorn of the peoples or cause your nation to fall, declares the Sovereign LORD."

Ezekiel 36:15 (NIV)

"They loathed all food and drew near the gates of death."

Psalm 107:18 (NIV)

****

"And you, son of man, on the day I take away their stronghold, their joy and glory, the delight of their eyes, their heart's desire, and their sons and daughters as well."

Ezekiel 24:25 (NIV)

****

"I delight greatly in the LORD; my soul rejoices in my God. For he has clothed me with garments of salvation and arrayed me in a robe of his righteousness, as a bridegroom adorns his head like a priest, and as a bride adorns herself with her jewels."

Isaiah 61:10 (NIV)

****

"None of the remnant of Judah who have gone to live in Egypt will escape or survive to return to the land of Judah, to which

they long to return and live; none will return except a few fugitives."

Jeremiah 44:14 (NIV)

****

CHAPTER TWO

Your Current Narrative

Chapter Two
YOUR CURRENT NARRATIVE

"Man is nothing else but what he purposes; he exists only in so far as he realizes himself; he is therefore nothing else but **the sum of his actions,** *nothing else but what his life is."*

Jean-Paul Sartre

Your narrative is your story, the story of your life. Each day, you add a page to your story. How is that done? It is done by simply living your life as it has come to be designed. Do you realize your life is a stage play and every new season in your life is a different act or a different scene in the play? It's true. The world is a stage, and on it, we perform. We either perform as someone directs us, or we perform at our own direction, or we perform by the leading of the Holy Spirit. Who has directed your narrative up to this point in your life?

Are you satisfied with where you are, or have you come to a point in your life where you are desperate for change? Maybe you desire change in one particular area or maybe you desire to have a complete overhaul of your life (which, of course, is an extreme desire that may take an exorbitant amount of time to bring to pass). Regardless of the specific area(s) you desire change in, before you can successfully move forward and effectuate change, there are two things you must consider and to which you must commit. Both stages are essential to effectuating change in your narrative.

First, you must be willing to undergo self-exploration, which requires self-love. "Self-love is a state of appreciation for oneself that grows from actions that support our physical, psychological, and spiritual growth. Self-love means having a high regard for your own well-being and happiness. Self-love means taking care of your own needs and not sacrificing your well-being to please others" (Brain & Behavior Research Foundation, 2022).

Self-love will permit you to delve into yourself to examine your makeup without condemnation from what you may uncover or rediscover. One of the things you may learn is the role *you* played in specific events, where in the past you may have pointed an accusatory finger at someone else. Also, you may learn that you possess specific character traits that may not particularly appeal to you today. It is possible at one point in your life, maybe during a time of crisis, you developed the trait, but now you no longer desire the trait to be part of your character. For example, maybe you were a victim of sexual assault at a young age, and as a result of the victimization, you developed a mean streak. You did so to present yourself as a tough person who would not be victimized again. As a person who is now a bit older, you can let go of the tough exterior and allow the authentic you to be seen without fear of being victimized.

During the self-exploration, you may uncover weaknesses you possess, which contributed to downfalls or failures you experienced. For example, maybe you love sweets and find them difficult to resist. You were on a weight-loss plan, and you were doing well by staying focused on your goal. One day, things took a turn. When you were watching a cooking television show, the contestants were making a holiday meal, and you were introduced to a scrumptious-looking desert. You decided you would prepare it for your family as a special treat. Once you took one small harmless bite, you were hooked. Your sweet tooth took over, and you continued preparing the desert once a week for Sunday dinner. From there, the weight-loss plan went out the window, and you have not looked back since. That was twenty pounds ago.

The purpose of self-exploration is to journey to the path of liberation. According to the Oxford Dictionary, liberation is "the act of setting someone free from imprisonment, slavery, and oppression." In this case, the person you are setting free is you. You deserve to be set free from the entrapment of your own walls. Changing your narrative consists of tearing down pre-constructed walls. These walls may have served as a sense of protection from past hurts.

However, think about walls that surround a structure. Those same walls that are designed to protect those inside the walls also serve as a barrier to keep foreign entities that exist on the outside from entering. In the case of walls that fortify us that were built from past experiences, those walls not only keep everything inside that we allowed into our personal space, but they also keep everything outside, including harmful substances and people as well as beneficial substances and people. As we self-explore, we decide which character traits we want to maintain and those we want to excavate and eliminate.

Secondly, you must take a look backward to see which agents caused the particular undesirable effects, landing you in your current position(s) of desiring change. Please note, looking back into your past will be a momentary venture. How long the moment lasts will be different for each individual and is typically predicated upon the age of the person. The older one is, the more years the person has to "look" through. However, the types of activities in which the person has engaged can also dictate how much time the "look" will require.

The trip down memory lane is necessary to provide insight into the events that transpired early on in your life, which directly impact your present-day experiences and conditions.

"Brethren, I count not myself to have apprehended: but this one thing I do, forgetting those things which are behind, and reaching forth unto those things which are before, I press toward the mark for the prize of the high calling of God in Christ Jesus."

Philippians 3:13-14 (KJV)

In these verses, Apostle Paul eloquently admonishes us to not hold tightly to the past: past failures, past hurts, past mistakes, past disappointments, past losses, etc. Therefore, to "look back" is to glance back in an effort to ascertain something, not to become transfixed (focused for a prolonged period of time). Furthermore, "please keep in mind that in Bible terminology, 'to forget' does not mean 'to fail to remember.' Apart from senility, hypnosis, or a brain malfunction, no mature person can forget what has happened in the past. We may wish that we could erase certain bad memories, but we cannot. 'To forget' in the Bible means 'no longer to be influenced by or affected by'" (Wiersbe, 2007, p. 648).

Consider this, for a driver, the vehicle being driven must be equipped with the necessary tools, including side view mirrors and a rearview mirror. If a driver does not employ all the provided tools and decides to only look through the front windshield while driving and gives no concern to what is occurring on either side or behind the vehicle, the driver could soon become engaged in a traffic collision. A safe, conscientious driver takes precautions by using all available windows and mirrors, by turning his head to view traffic, pedestrians, and parked cars on all sides of his moving vehicle. This safe practice of driving includes glancing in the rearview mirror and side view mirrors to see who or what may be approaching from the rear. The driver does not watch continuously in the rearview mirror, but to be aware of anything that may be transpiring that could indeed impact his very near future, he checks it often.

Another example is that of a runner who is involved in a relay race. A relay race is comprised of four runners per team. Once the starting pistol is fired, runner one begins running the race with the baton in hand. As she approaches runner two, runner two begins to sprint with her head slightly turned toward runner one who is obviously behind her. She keeps her head in that position until the baton has safely been passed into her hand. From the moment she receives the baton until she hands the baton to runner three, she is strictly facing forward. What may occur behind her has no further bearing on the race at hand. If she were to look back, she could be thrown off course. She could stumble. She could run past runner three without handing off the baton. A number of things could occur if she were to get off focus.

From these examples, we understand looking back has the advantage of knowing what has transpired to determine the possible impacts on the future. Concurrently, we understand we are not to become transfixed on the past. We look into the past to learn how to have a better present and future. Once you look back into your past and gather the information you require to detect behavioral patterns and various events, then you can focus on all that lies ahead for you.

Let's take a moment to examine the opening quote for this chapter: *"Man is nothing else but what he purposes; he exists only in so far as he realizes himself; he is therefore nothing else but* ***the sum of his actions****, nothing else but what his life is."* Jean-

Paul Sartre asserted this statement in the mid-1900s. While I do not agree with most of Sartre's philosophical assertions, which are deeply rooted in his atheistic beliefs, I do agree with his postulation regarding man and his experiences to a great degree. Allow me to explain.

In the 17th century, John Locke, an empiricist (a person who supports the theory that all knowledge is based on experience derived from the senses), re-affirmed the theory of "tabula rasa," which is a Latin term for "clean slate." In epistemology (theory of knowledge) and psychology (the scientific study of the human mind and its functions, especially those affecting behavior in a given context), tabula rasa is a supposed condition that empiricists have attributed to the human mind (the mind of a newborn baby) before ideas have been imprinted on it by the reaction of the senses to the external world of objects (Britannica, 2022). This theory is not as cut and dry as it sounds. Allow me to add this: a newborn baby does have memory to a certain degree. Studies have shown a baby recognizes his/her mother's voice. The point here is the mind of a newborn is without real-world experiences that resulted from tangible interactions but are not necessarily void of any memory. Other than voice recognition, there are no experiences from which to gain memories for a newborn child.

In *An Essay Concerning Human Understanding* (1690), John Locke argued for the mind's initial resemblance to "white paper, void of all characters," with "all the *materials* of reason and knowledge" derived from experience that would occur later. Locke did *not* believe, however, that the mind is literally blank or empty prior to experience, and almost no other empiricist has taken such an extreme position. Locke himself acknowledged an innate power of "reflection" (awareness of one's own ideas, sensations, emotions, and so on) as a means of exploiting the materials given by experience as well as a limited realm of a priori (nonexperiential) knowledge, which he nevertheless regarded as "trifling" and essentially empty of content (Britannica, 2022).

From that same disposition of the human mind posited by John Locke, Jean-Paul Sartre postulated his own ideas of man and his experiences. Sartre believed humans were born with a mind that did not contain memory because there were no lived experiences from which to draw. According to Sartre's theory, memory is formed through lived events. Once a person has experiences, those very experiences and the memories of them shapes who the person becomes. That belief is the premise for which the information in this chapter will be based upon.

A familiar passage in the Bible is:

"For as he thinketh within himself, so is he.."

Psalm 23:7a (ASV)

When David wrote these words, there was much hidden meaning within them other than what simply rests upon the surface of the words. According to Gill's Exposition of the Entire Bible (1748-63), David was implying, "He is not the man his mouth speaks or declares him to be, but what his heart thinks; which is discovered by his looks and actions, and by which he is to be judged of, and not by his words." David was warning us to be careful about receiving one's words as an honest interpretation of the person. Rather, we are to discern the true nature of the person by watching the actions performed. The actions performed reveal what is in a person's heart, and one's intent cannot be hidden from a discerning spirit.

That raises two important questions: From where does a person's actions originate? What is the starting point of an action? The answer to both is revealed in the verse. *"As a man thinks in his heart..."* Notice the word *"thinks."* Then, notice <u>where</u> the man is thinking- in his heart. So, it is the thoughts a person holds dear, which emanate from his heart, that precipitates an action. Jeremiah 17:9 (NLT) says, *"The human heart is the most deceitful of all things, and desperately wicked. Who really knows how bad it is?"* Given what we understand, we can readily surmise the following: the natural sequence of events is first there is a *thought.* Then, the thought is followed by an *action.* The action is then followed by a corresponding *reaction*. The collection of actions and reactions form experiences.

Do our experiences shape who we are? Are the memories we keep from these experiences more important in shaping who we are than the experiences themselves? Many scholars believe our experiences *do* shape who we are and that the memories of those experiences are equally as important. Every experience we have shapes who we are in one way or another. *Every experience!* Even an unmonumental experience will change or impact us, even if the impact is subtle. Small impacts coupled together can cause a greater change or shift.

A seemingly unimportant experience may simply change how you feel one day, which can cause a chain reaction of how you act a certain day, and how you act that day could affect your life as a whole. The reaction can be similar to what is known as the domino effect, which is the cumulative effect produced when one event triggers a chain of similar events, whether negative or positive. Those actions and experiences shape our identity. Therefore, our identity is simply a collection of the moments and happenings of our lives. Some experiences are more prominent and influential than others, but they all play a role in shaping our thoughts and behaviors.

Daniel Kahneman (2000), a modern-day philosopher, believes experience and memory both shape who we are in different ways. He believes there is an "experiencing self who lives in the present and knows the present" and there is a "remembering self that keeps score and maintains the story of our life." Overall, he says, "What we get to keep from our experiences is a story." This idea is what ties experience to memory and vice versa. Experiences and memories are both equally important in shaping who we are.

Therefore, it is important we dedicate time surveying both our experiences and our memories of those experiences, while being mindful that memories do have a tendency to fade over time. That is why when we recall events we experienced with other people, they may remember some details one way, and we may remember them slightly differently. We all have our version of the "truth." And, it is our version of the truth that we often re-tell ourselves, and possibly others, and our reality is what impacts us.

The following example will demonstrate the point I am making about our version of the truth and the impact it can have on us.

> When Melvin was seven years old, he was at a park playing on the jungle gym with his older brother and some friends. As he was running around playing, he suddenly felt a push from behind. The push caused Melvin to quickly sprawl to the ground. He attempted to break the fall with his hands, but as he felt himself quickly approaching the sand, his small hands could not break his fall because they entered the gritty and crunchy sand that was beneath him. With the landing was a loud bang as Melvin's face hit the edge of the slide.
>
> Before he could collect himself, he heard a roar of laughter coming from behind him. Horrified from the pain he felt radiating from his mouth, he turned to see his brother and one of the other boys standing behind him. One look at Melvin and the laughter halted just as quickly as it had begun. Clearing the fog from his eyes by a quick shake of his head, he noticed them pointing at him with looks of bewilderment filling their eyes. Melvin's brother went over to help him while saying, "You're bleeding." Tears sprang from Melvin's eyes because the pain was so

unbearable and also from the humiliation he felt from being in the presence of the other boys. Back at home, his mother cleaned his mouth and noticed one of his front teeth was not only loose, but it was chipped as well.

Years later, Melvin had been wearing a smile with a chipped tooth and had been teased for that chipped tooth off and on. The teasing always bothered him, and it caused a bit of animosity between him and his brother because Melvin had always blamed him for the fall.

The way Melvin's brother remembers it, however, does not align with Melvin's memory. From adolescence, through his teenage years, to adulthood, Melvin carried the scars (mentally and physically) from that day, and they impacted the way he saw his brother and ultimately how he responded to him. From his brother's perspective, his love for Melvin had not wavered in the least.

From this example, we can see that varying perspectives yield different responses.

With everything that has been discussed over the last few pages, we are now ready to take that momentary trip down memory lane to survey our past experiences. Let's begin with childhood patterns and experiences. As you read, reflect upon your adolescent and pre-teenage years. Take note of your varied experiences and the impact and impression of those experiences upon your life. Do not discount any occurrence as they all have value and have left an imprint upon you.

Childhood Patterns and Experiences

As children grow and development through adolescence into adulthood, everything they experience will determine the type of adult they will become: what they engage in, the family and friends they are surrounded by, their education, what they see, what they hear, how they internalize the world around them, etc. Below are a few areas that directly impact children, either positively or negatively and sometimes both.

Affection

Children who are raised by parents who, despite their busy, stressful lives that are filled with endless concerns, take time to dine with them, engage in daily activity, converse with and embrace them will lead healthier lives. These children will have a "higher self-esteem, improved academic performance, better child-parent communication, and fewer psychological and behavior problems" (The Gottman Institute, 2022). Furthermore, these children will also be comfortable with receiving affection from others (particularly in adulthood) as well as giving it, during all phases of their lives.

"On the other hand, children who do not have affectionate parents tend to have lower self-esteem and feel more alienated, hostile, aggressive, and anti-social" (The Gottman Institute, 2022). Additionally, children reared in homes where there is a lack of affection tend to become affectionally rigid and may become socially awkward in situations that require individuals to be in close proximity to others. A study conducted by Duke University Medical School found babies with very affectionate and attentive mothers grow up to be happier, more resilient, and less-anxious adults (The Gottman Institute).

Read the following examples that share two different experiences for newborn children and the impact affection has on their lives.

> From the moment Rebecca and Paul learned they were pregnant, they began rubbing Rebecca's stomach, massaging their baby. As the baby grew, in utero, they began singing songs

and even made up a few of their own just for their child. They had heard babies can hear while in the womb, and they wanted their child to know their voices and hopefully be able to recognize them after making her entrance into the world. Once their daughter, who they named Stephanie, was born, they took turns holding, changing, dressing, and feeding her all while being gentle and loving.

Rebecca and Paul's earnest desire was for Stephanie to feel loved and secure. They wanted her to grow up feeling self-confident and safe even in a world that presents danger and harm all around. From those first few months until the day their daughter left for college, Rebecca and Paul nurtured their daughter. When Stephanie gave birth to a son years later, everything that was demonstrated towards her was in turn demonstrated towards her son, and he grew up as a well-adjusted child who was loved by his parents and grandparents, feeling love, warmth, and security.

Felicity and Trevor were preparing to give birth to twins, which had taken them both completely by surprise because neither of them had twins on their side of the family. Then, to compound matters, Felicity ended up having a rough pregnancy due to various medical conditions and was placed on bed rest for the last six months of the pregnancy. Her medical condition led to a severe drop in income for the household because her employer could not hold her job during her absence. Trevor was then required to carry the financial load for the family, which caused undue pressure upon him, especially because he had to withdraw from the college courses in which he was enrolled. He needed to spend the hours he would have been in class working the newly acquired part-time job he had been fortunate enough to obtain. With the unexpected changes, both Felicity and Trevor felt the stress, and Felicity fell into depression as she watched her husband come home tired day after day.

When the twins, Sylvia and Shawn, were born, they cried a lot and had colic. The sounds of their cries caused Felicity to fall into post-partum depression, leaving much of the twins' care to her mother who had come to assist. With all Felicity and Trevor had experienced prior to the birth of their children and directly afterward, they did not form a nurturing bond with Sylvia and Shawn although they loved them dearly. The lack of intimacy between the children and their parents caused a continuous irritability throughout their toddler and adolescent years and impacted their schooling.

Teasing

Children who suffer teasing and mocking, whether in the home, neighborhood, or classroom, "can be left with long-lasting emotional scars" while other children are able to overcome the momentary effects of teasing (Sherwood, 2017). The emotional scars can affect both present behavior as well as increase the risks for psychological and academic hardships throughout school and into adulthood. Teasing can impact self-esteem (causing it to drop or fail to develop to a healthy level), cause depression and anxiety, impact academic performance (leading to lower grades), and create a bully or a class clown.

Conversely, children who are consistently praised and encouraged on a regular basis will develop healthy levels of confidence, security, and an outgoing personality. In turn, they will be more apt to encourage others by praising them with compliments and words of encouragement. All children will undergo teasing to one degree or another, and the teasing will impact them differently. Because the impact of teasing upon a specific child is uncertain, it is best to keep the teasing to a minimum, preventing long-lasting negative effects.

Read the following example as an illustration of the aforementioned perspectives.

Sabrina was a fun-loving child from birth to five years old when she entered kindergarten. Sabrina was a bit overweight, and some of her classmates teased her nearly every day while she was at school. The friends she had made begun to stay clear of her because other students had begun to tease them just because they were Sabrina's friends. Thankfully, there was one brave soul who decided to continue his friendship with Sabrina regardless of what the insensitive bullies said or did. His name was Tommy. No matter what was said or done to Sabrina, Tommy was by her side. At times, Tommy would stand up for Sabrina. Other times, he advised her to ignore the comments that were tossed her way. When the teasing shifted in his direction, Tommy stood tall and spoke up and defended himself, refusing to succumb to the bullies' taunts.

Over time, the bullies grew tired of the teasing, and some of them began to back off. Although they were only five years old just like the rest of the kindergartners, their words hurt Sabrina, and each night, she cried at dinner when her parents asked about her day at school. Before the teasing began to wane off, Sabrina no longer had joy when it was time to go to school. But Sabrina had many people surrounding her, and they all loved her.

One of the persons in her circle of life was her older brother Tim, who was in third grade. Tim had heard the details of the teasing his sister had endured in the kindergarten area, and his heart grew heavy daily when he heard the reports. After school, Tim made it his mission to make his sister feel better. He hugged Sabrina and wiped her tears while telling her how pretty she was. Sabrina would smile and feel warmth in her heart. Eventually, Sabrina began to tune out the voices of the naysayers, choosing to receive the positive words instead. From there, she developed into a healthy young lady even though she endured teasing from time to time just like all children do.

Verbal Abuse

Verbal abuse is the use of harsh, hurtful language while communicating with people. Abusive words, including swear words, ones that inflict pain, negative labels and put downs, are aggressive in nature. Verbal abuse is associated with the following behaviors: insulting, yelling, nagging, criticizing, belittling, undermining, swearing, and threatening. The effects of verbal abuse include changes in the developing brain (for children under eighteen); destruction of self-confidence; development of an inferiority complex;

increases the risk of substance abuse; depression; negative effects on one's physical health; and increases abusive tendencies in the victims.

Conversely, children who experience non-abusive and non-aggressive environments have a much higher opportunity for proper brain development through its various stages; healthier self-confidence; higher self-worth and personal value; lower risk of substance abuse; stable moods and anxiety level; good physical health conditions; and lower risk of abusive tendencies.

Here are a few examples of statements that constitute verbal abuse:

- "You're ugly/stupid/useless."
- "You'll never amount to anything."
- "You were incredibly rude to me." (when you did nothing wrong)
- "Disrespect me one more time, and I'll hurt you."
- "Your mother doesn't really love you." (said by an abusive father)
- "I wish I never had you."
- "You ruined my life."
- "Don't fucking talk to me."
- "Shut your mouth, or I'll tape it shut."
- "You're dressed like a whore."
- "Why are you so goddamn weak?"

- "Can't you ever do anything right?"
- "You're being bullied at school because you've done something to deserve it, so don't come to me moaning about it."
- "Do that again, and I will hand you over for adoption."
- "You are a disgrace to this family."
- "Why can't you be more like your sister/ brother? Why do you have to be such a loser?"
- "You're not having a birthday party this year because you don't deserve one."

Signs of verbal abuse include:

- Excessive criticism
- Invalidating emotions
- Name-calling
- Making jokes at your expense
- Yelling, screaming, and swearing
- Constant comparisons to others
- Threatening to hurt you
- Blaming you for things that are out of your control
- Shaming or humiliating you in front of others
- Verbal aggression

All of the forms of abuse described above (and other forms), when issued out in continuous doses, can and will have a negative impact on a child's life and on into adulthood unless the child undergoes counseling to heal from the scars. Furthermore, a child does not need to suffer abuse in all areas to endure life-alerting damage. Suffering abuse in one area is enough to commit a lifetime of damage.

Educational Influences

Let's shift our focus from home life and social environments to the structured environment of education. Education consumes half of a child's waking hours, and as such, that is where most of their self-esteem and confidence is shaped, from the ages of five to eighteen. In school, children are impacted by the words and actions of their teachers, peers, friends, other students in various grades, and other adults, such as school staff and personnel (principal, secretary, aides, nurse, etc.) and their peers' parents. According to Akin and Radford (2018), relationships with peers, family, and teachers influence the development of students' self-esteem.

Educators can create positive learning environments to build and support student self-esteem and resilience (the capability to face challenges), which contribute to positive mental health and student academic and social success. Youth resilience factors include intrapersonal, interpersonal, and community experiences. Teacher actions, and interactions, within the learning environment influence the development of student self-esteem and resiliency within students (Akin & Radford, 2018) by not only using positive language, but also by engaging students in activities that demonstrate their strengths and serve to strengthen their weaknesses.

When children possess low self-esteem, some signs they may demonstrate include:

- Fear of failing or hesitance in situations that may end in embarrassment
- Lack of interest or motivation, even in things that used to get them excited
- Avoiding new situations or having a fear of trying new things
- Trouble in making friends
- Quickly frustrated when things become difficult

(GoGuardian Team, 2018)

Low self-esteem can arise in students early through everyday situations or troubling experiences. Causes of low self-esteem include:

- Lack of consistent parental support
- Feeling like no one is there to help them academically

- Bullying by classmates or older students
- A traumatic experience happened to them at some point
- Not feeling like their skills can match up with other students

(GoGuardian Team, 2018).

For children to thrive emotionally, physically, psychologically, and educationally once they matriculate into high school and from there into the world of adulthood, they must have a healthy foundation in place long before that time arrives.

During the teenage years and young adult years, everything that is experienced either compounds and solidifies what occurred the fourteen years before or begins to smooth out some of the rough edges and allow healthier experiences to occur. As mentioned earlier, it is the relationships and interactions the individual has with others that will greatly impact the life canvas that is being written upon.

What is newly introduced in this chapter of life is typically long-lasting relationships with others that can greatly impact the person's future ideologies. These relationships are typically emotionally and physically driven.

High school leads directly into college and/or the workforce (sometimes both), so if one's self-esteem is low during these four years, it could greatly affect a student's future. Here are a few main signs of low self-esteem to be aware of that could be present in high school students:

- Constantly pointing the finger at others for mistakes
- Lack of interest at both home and school
- Continuous negativity
- Feeling like nobody cares
- Persistently feeling anxious or sad

(GoGuardian Team, 2018)

There can be several reasons why a high school student is struggling with low self-esteem. It can often seem to go hand-in-hand with being a teenager.

- Unfortunately, bullying is quite common in high school and can greatly affect the student for years to come.
- Abuse at home can bring on a lifetime of low self-esteem.
- Changing schools during high school years can be a traumatic event resulting in problems with confidence.
- Mood disorders with unpredictable hormones.
- An unsupportive family can bring on a feeling of worthlessness.

(GoGuardian Team, 2018)

The effect of low self-esteem can inhibit a student's teenage years significantly. It may bring on:

- An early use of alcohol and problems with drugs
- No interest in pursuing their education
- Poor self-image problems
- Negativity
- Trouble sustaining relationships

(GoGuardian Team, 2018)

Now that you have read the last few sections and as you prepare to read through the next few, pay close attention and see what resonates with you. How was your self-esteem as you transitioned from elementary school to middle or junior high school and then into senior high school? How was your self-esteem when you transitioned from high school to college or into the job market?

Relational Impacts

According to Hongfei, King and Chi (2012), individuals can achieve a sense of self-worth through their personal attributes (personal self-esteem), relationship with significant others (relational self-esteem), or social group membership (collective self-esteem). Authors Harris and Orth (2019) are in agreement as their research yielded similar findings: "positive social relationships, social support and social acceptance help shape the development of self-esteem in people over time across ages 4 to 76." Furthermore, their research "findings suggest that the link between people's social relationships and their level of self-esteem is truly reciprocal in all developmental stages across the life span" (Harris & Orth).

Relationships impact all parties involved. If the relationship is healthy, and the participants treat each other with love and kindness, demonstrated by their words and actions, positive self-esteem levels will be fostered. Conversely, if relationships are filled with angst, concern, stress, frustration, and harsh words, the impact on the participants' self-esteem can be devastating, depending on how long the person engages in the relationship. The type of relationships a person engages in can set patterns for their life, and those patterns can be difficult to break.

Employment Impacts

Earlier, I mentioned children spend half of their waking hours at school. The same is true regarding people in the workforce. Therefore, "as most people spend a large part of their waking hours working, there is reason to expect that the work domain affects how individuals think and feel about themselves. Experiences at work, such as job success and failure, being promoted or dismissed, and having good or bad work conditions may shape self-esteem" (Krauss & Orth, 2022).

Let's examine how one's employment may impact one's self esteem. "The work domain offers the opportunity to achieve ambitions, to perceive self-competence, and to feel proud of oneself. Taking on responsibility as an employee may also help to develop a more mature personality and feel better about oneself. Maybe most importantly, the job lets people experience that they are socially included and accepted, both within and outside the workplace. Perceiving that one is valued by others may greatly help to value oneself. Thus, the work domain may affect self-esteem in several ways" (Krauss & Orth, 2022).

At the same time, those who already possess a high or healthy self-esteem will go into the workplace already feeling self-confident, thereby impacting the workplace. "People with high self-esteem believe in themselves and might therefore select a job with more responsibility and autonomy compared with people with low self-esteem. Choosing a work environment that suits one's own personality, including self-esteem, may lead to more motivation, better job performance, and more job satisfaction. In addition, self-esteem may shape how people cope under stressful circumstances and how they perceive their work environment" (Krauss & Orth, 2022).

"Moreover, self-esteem affects social interactions. For example, people with high self-esteem tend to engage in more open behaviors to improve connectedness, whereas people with low self-esteem sometimes behave distant to protect themselves from being rejected. Consequently, people with high self-esteem are more likely to succeed in building and maintaining positive social relationships at work, to receive more social support by coworkers and supervisors, and, ultimately, to be more successful at work" (Krauss & Orth, 2022).

Conjoining both perspectives, it is certainly possible that work experiences influence people's self-esteem and that, vice versa, self-esteem influences work experiences. Importantly, we individually must assess the condition in which we enter into the workplace as well as the condition of the workplace and how it fosters self-esteem, personal growth in various areas, and interpersonal relationships.

As you read the sections on *The Impact of Words* and *Conditioning*, reflect upon how those subjects make meaning for you while you continue to survey your past.

The impact of words

When a child is harassed by a bully who spouts insults and expletives, a popular phrase to respond with is, "Sticks and stones may break my bones, but words will never hurt me." And, the child who utters those words does so with the hope that the words will render truth in his/her life even though times have undoubtedly proved differently. By the time the child reaches adulthood, he/she has learned that merely speaking the words of the popular phrase does not make them true.

As adults, from our own experiences with other people, we understand words *can* be hurtful. Sometimes, the damage we have sustained or inflicted upon others is far worse than that of sticks and stones. However, even with this truth, as children and adults we still speak without considering the impact our words will have in a person's life.

In a moment's notice, we have at times flown off the handle without stopping to think about the consequences of what we are about to say. Other times, we react to something someone said or did and start attacking that person with cruel accusations or vicious threats. The damage of our words could be so profound, and the damage could forever sever a personal relationship we have with a person or cause a lasting strain. Flying off the handle without stopping to think about the repercussions will lead to people getting hurt, and later, people will be sorry for what they said. But, unfortunately, the damage will be done.

Author Yehuda Berg (2021) states, "Words are singularly the most powerful force available to humanity. Words have energy and power with the ability to help, to heal, to hurt, to harm, to humiliate and to humble." Berg's perspective is corroborated by James 3:8-12 (NIV), which informs us, *"No human being can tame the tongue. It is a restless evil, full of deadly poison. With the tongue we praise our Lord and Father, and with it we curse human beings, who have been made in God's likeness. Out of the same mouth come praise and cursing. My brothers and sisters, this should not be. Can both fresh water and salt water flow from the same spring? My brothers and sisters, can a fig tree bear olives, or a grapevine bear figs? Neither can a salt spring produce fresh water."*

The words we choose and how we choose to use them can build others up or tear them down; they can bring a community together or rip it apart; they can breed joy or discontentment. For as the Bible says, *"Death and life are in the power of the tongue"* (Proverbs 18:21, KJV). We should ask ourselves,

"What is my objective when I speak? To build or to tear down?" Additionally, we should ask ourselves, "How do I prefer others to speak to me?" Our answer to that question should dictate how we should in turn speak to others. After all, the Bible instructs in Matthew 22:39 (NKJV), *"And the second is like it: 'You shall love your neighbor a yourself'."* Basically, we should do unto others as we would have them do unto us.

Choose the words you will speak very carefully because they have the potential of accomplishing nearly anything or destroying nearly anything. Just one negative comment can ruin a person's day. A few might even ruin the person's life. On the flip side, one positive and encouraging comment can be just enough to increase personal engagement, create healthier cultures, and make more of a difference in an individual's life than you will ever know. Our words are powerful and should be treated with respect.

Let's examine how words can impact people and why words should be chosen wisely to eliminate heartache and suffering and instead germinate life, encouragement, peace, and hope. As you read the next several sections, assess how your parents' words and words of other authority figures impacted you as you were growing up, while you were in school, as you worked on various jobs, and also assess words spoken by those you engaged with in relationships.

Words are powerful!

One of the greatest mistakes we can make is believing our words have no impact or weight in other people's lives. This is a misnomer many people hold. Within the words we speak is an emotional potency. Each word we use or hear can have a colossal impact. Never think of words as inconsequential. Instead, think of them as powerful. Words can build up or tear down. They can motivate or discourage. They can empower or weaken.

Even if people pretend to ignore our words (and they often do) or we pretend to ignore theirs, can a person actually unhear what has been said? Of course not! People do not suddenly become deaf when someone is speaking to them. And no matter if they tell us our opinion is of no consequence or our perspective is a nonfactor, they still hear us when we speak, and we hear them as well.

Put yourself in someone else's position for just a moment. Recall a heated conversation you had with someone. Can you still remember the person's words practically verbatim even years down the road? Now consider a similar conversation in someone else's life. Your words could be the ones *he/she* has in *his/her* head. Why is that? Because words sting, and they have lasting impressions. Most importantly, once words are spoken, they cannot be unspoken nor can they be unheard! No matter how much the speaker or the hearer may want that to be true.

The words we choose mean something. Whether that meaning is positive or negative is up to the speaker. If you want to live positively and make a positive, healthy impact in the world, try starting with the daily words you choose. How do you talk to others, to yourself, to your superiors, and to your inferiors? When we recognize the value our words have, we take the first step in bettering our community, our workplaces, our homes, our temperaments, and our dispositions by disarming ourselves of words that breed hatred, discontentment, anger, strife, bitterness, jealousy, and envy.

Again, life and death are in the power of your tongue (Proverbs 18:21). Render life unto those with whom you come in contact by thinking before you speak just as you desire for them to do for you. And, if someone speaks to you in an undesirable manner, address the person and have a conversation about your perspective. This is the best way to halt unwanted aggression or negativity from people by way of the words they choose to use when conversing with you.

Words are remembered.

If words have meaning, then they are definitely remembered. Consider the child in class whose teacher tells him he is never going to be as good a student as his older sister. This comment, which could mean nothing to the teacher, may always be remembered by the child and viewed as a statement of disappointment. Unknowingly, the child could inadvertently decide not to try to improve his scholastic skillset and/or the child could begin to resent his older sister.

In contrast, think of the child whose teacher tells him how much she believes in him. Even a simple comment can forever make an impact to either uplift or defeat. To live a positive and impactful life is to recognize our words are not just for today. Even though they may be spoken today, they will continue to live on every day after today. What you say today could be remembered for years to come, so choose your words carefully. The best way to do that is to stop and think before you speak. Be mindful of those who will hear your words. Consider how the words will impact them.

Let's test this out. Think about someone who was influential in your life, someone who made an impact. How did the person impact your life? What did the person *do* that impacted you? What did the person *say*? How long ago was it? Notice how you still remember what was said or done. You may not remember word for word, but you have a sense of what was said or done. More importantly, you know how the words or actions made you feel.

Words make a difference.

Words... are... powerful! Think of powerful words throughout history, which have made a lasting difference in our world. *"Four score and seven years ago." "I have a dream." "Tear down this wall."* Our words, when chosen correctly, can make a positive contribution in our own lives and the lives of those around us.

Words filter through us and seep into our community, where they are absorbed then reasserted by others to people they know. When we recognize the power our words have, we see the impact they can have, and we should choose them based on what kind of difference we want to make. Furthermore, by choosing our words carefully in front of our youth can save generations to come by depositing positivity instead of negativity and by eliminating words that divide, conquer, defeat, separate, spurn, isolate, degrade, debilitate, and maim.

Remember, words have the ability to shape a person's character, integrity, and thought processes. With that in mind, think about the impact words have on children who have young impressionable minds. Not only do they hear words that shape who they are on a daily basis, but oftentimes they will rehearse either verbally or mentally what was said to them over the years. Children do not usually have the power to shut down negative words, as they are spoken at the will of the speaker who may be another child but in most cases is an adult. As a result, they begin to internalize the words they hear repeatedly and conceptualize the words as truth for their life. The same is true for adults. They too internalize words spoken by others, especially those for which they have a great deal of respect.

For example, if a parent consistently tells a child, "You can achieve any goal you set your mind to," the child will eventually internalize the affirmation and believe it to be true. If that child hears the same affirmation from various individuals, it will be reaffirmed with greater intensity. I have first-hand experience with receiving positive affirmations throughout my life, from childhood to adulthood, and they have created a healthy self-esteem within me. Because of that, I have set goals and worked hard to achieve them, even if at times I felt doing so was against great odds. However, because of the self-belief that was instilled in me early on, I did not and do not allow challenges to deter me. Understandably, however, that is not true for all children or adults.

Consider the child who grew up repeatedly hearing, "You are never going to amount to anything." The child's hopes were blasted before he even knew how to hope. And, if those negative words were fortified by others, he at some point began to internalize those words, making them true in his psyche. Then, unfortunately, those words will play out in his life because he believed what he was told by unloving adults who pierced his heart.

(Special note- this entire section on *The Impact of Words* was excerpted from ***Pearls of Wisdom*** (White-Elliott, 2022) with minor changes and/or additions.)

CONDITIONING

The result of experiencing the same treatment (positive or negative stimuli), such as repeatedly hearing accolades or harsh words, re-affirming expressions or being verbally abused, being encouraged and pushed to achieve goals or being turned down and discouraged and then developing a response to that treatment is what psychologists refer to as Classical Conditioning, which is "learning through association and was discovered by Ivan Pavlov, a Russian physiologist. In simple terms, two stimuli are linked together to produce a new learned response in a person or animal" (Simply Psychology, 2021). Conditional theories based on stimulus and response are grounded in the assumption that human behavior is learned.

Pavlov's theory was grounded in the evidence he gained from experimenting with dogs. "He showed that dogs could be conditioned to salivate at the sound of a bell if that sound was repeatedly presented at the same time that they were given food. First the dogs were presented with the food, they salivated. The food was the unconditioned stimulus and salivation was an unconditioned (innate) response" (Simply Psychology, 2021).

All mammals can be conditioned to respond in specific manners, including humans. When children (or any person) have been accustomed to receiving particular stimuli, such as specific words or actions, they usually form a pattern of responding in a specific manner, i.e. crying, laughing, smiling, growing quiet, and even bedwetting.

For example- When a child is disciplined, whether in an appropriate or inappropriate manner, the child will respond because as a whole, children do not enjoy discipline. They would rather run wild and do any and everything they choose. However, good parenting includes disciplining children. A child who is disciplined by getting slapped across the face will begin flinching every time the disciplining parent raises his hand, even if the hand is being raised for something else. Flinching becomes a natural response to the lifted hand. The purpose of discipline is not to instill fear but to correct a behavior. In this example, fear has been instilled and has resulted in an undesired response.

Conversely, children respond to other stimuli as well. Take my youngest granddaughter Zuri for example. When she comes to visit, I prefer her to eat in her high chair to keep messes to a minimum. (Note- she is two years old.) After preparing her food, I pull the high chair from its stored location to a place more comfortable, usually in front of the television where her favorite show is playing. When Zuri notices me going toward her chair and pulling it out, she automatically comes over and stands right next to it and begins making certain motions while smiling at me. (Note- She loves to eat.)

Once I put her chair in position, she raises her arms for me to lift her and place her into the chair. Usually, I tell her it is time to eat as I am moving the chair, but even when I do not say those words, my movements tell her it is time to eat. My repeated action has conditioned her to know when it is time to eat, and she demonstrates her understanding by her responses.

As you can see, conditioning can have negative or positive effects. Just as we are conditioned by the people with whom we engage, we also condition others by our responses to them. It is a reciprocal action that typically occurs without warning.

Having discussed childhood patterns and experiences (affection, teasing, verbal abuse, educational influences); relational impacts; educational impacts; the impact of words; and conditioning, *our journey down memory lane has culminated.* Now that it is complete, I am sure you understand the purpose if you did not before. It was necessary to examine the causes of our current condition because in order to effectuate change, the causes needed to be ascertained and addressed. Simply understanding the effects of the causes and attempting to address them in a vacuum would prove futile. As Dr. Martin Luther King, Jr. stated in his infamous "Letter from Birmingham Jail," we should not be one "who looks merely at effects and does not grapple with the underlying causes."

Everything we have examined in this chapter makes it clear that we are not always in control of what we experience. And, because who we are is based upon our experiences, we are not completely in control of our identity, especially when another person may have usurped our agency over our choices. However, the responsibility for our life rests with us from the point we enter into adulthood (having the consciousness to reason and make wise decisions), and the responsibility remains with us until we depart this earth.

As Sartre says, "We are responsible for our 'world' as the horizon of meaning in which we operate and thus for everything in it insofar as their meaning and value are assigned by virtue of our life-orienting fundamental 'choice.'" Sartre believes that the fundamental "choice" (free will) is the basis of which our subsequent choices are made.

As an adult, you choose your own experiences (for the most part). Understand your decisions will affect all decisions you make afterwards and all experiences you will have afterwards; and by extension, those decisions will forever change your identity and who you will become. The ability to take control of your own identity and life is powerful and should not be ignored. It is important that you think of yourself as someone who can be shaped and changed. And, the power of shaping and changing should rest in your hands.

PART II

Your Transformation

Chapter Three

Transform Your Mind

Chapter Three
Transform Your Mind

"Do not be conformed to this world, but be transformed by the renewal of your mind, that by testing you may discern what is the will of God, what is good and acceptable and perfect."

Romans 12:2 (ESV)

Your greatest asset is your mind, for it is your strongest muscle. Just like all the other muscles in your body, you must exercise it properly in order to gain the best results and to delay or at least slow down the process of the loss of complete function. One way to keep your mind healthy and strong is to ensure positive thoughts are filtered into it on a regular basis. Because what goes in is what will come out.

Conversely, if you fail to guard your mind from negativity, you will find yourself on a destructive path, which can and will produce mental anguish, taxing the brain by causing it to work overtime, searching for solutions of reprieve. Therefore, you need to control your thoughts by not allowing them to become captive to or controlled by other people or entities or substances. When you relinquish, you give the people or substances power over your life (Adapted from White-Elliott, 2022).

Possessing complete power over your thoughts begins with choosing what type of mindset you will exercise on a daily basis. You can have a positive, strong mindset or a negative, corrupt mindset. The positive, strong mindset will greatly benefit you all the days of your life by allowing you to view life from a positive vantage point, seeing it to be full of opportunities and possibilities.

A negative, corrupt mindset will allow hurt to seep into your life and hinder any progress you attempt to make because you are anticipating negativity within every or most situations you encounter. It is true you cannot avoid ever being hurt, but how you view and deal with the hurt is what will determine the steps you take in overcoming the disappointment and pain.

To have fruitful and healthy outcomes in your life, you must set your mind in a prosperous direction by having a strong mindset geared toward positivity. Conversely, a negative mindset will not only impact your circumstances, but it will also impact your inner life. "You cannot have a positive life [with] a negative mind" (Meyer, 2011, p. 19).

"Bring[ing] about a change in the way [you] think [can] create happiness and a sense of fulfillment in [y]our life. A good thing about [the] brain is that it willingly adopts any changes that [you] bring about in [y]our thinking patterns" (Rishi, 2023).

"Change your thoughts
and you change your world."

Norman Vincent Peale

As you go through the process of transforming your mind, it is important to not concern yourself with the mindset of others.

"Never underestimate your power
to change yourself; never overestimate
your power to change others."

Wayne Dyer

It is essential to understand we all have a different disposition in life, as we are all products of our environment and circumstances. "Some people see things negatively because they have experienced unhappy circumstances all their lives and cannot imagine anything getting better. Then there are some people who see everything as bad and negative simply because that is the way they are on the inside. Whatever is the cause, a negative outlook leaves a person miserable and unlikely of making any progress toward [a better life]" (Meyer, 2011, p. 176).

I use the term "better life" to indicate life in a better state than its current state. But, a "better life" is subjective. It is relative to the person who is reading this book. What you may consider to be a better life for yourself may not be what the next person considers to be a better life. Actually, what you consider as a better life for yourself may only be a degree or two of separation from your current life. However, a "better life" may be ten degrees of separation for another person, thereby causing it to appear unfeasible (out of the realm of possibility) for him/her.

Beholding a different perspective is perfectly fine because your life situation is different from that of the next person. We each have to assess our life and make alterations accordingly, and our assessment cannot be measured by what others are doing or thinking. Gauging our life expectations based on the positionality of someone else's life can cause us to set our expectations too low or too high. Romans

12:3 (NIV) admonishes us, *"For by the grace given me I say to every one of you: Do not think of yourself more highly than you ought, but rather think of yourself with sober judgment, in accordance with the faith God has distributed to each of you."* Apostle Paul instructs us to be sober minded, not elevating ourselves in our own mind. Conversely, we should not mentally demote ourselves from where God has situated us. With that in mind, you are ready to move forward with your personal mental transformation.

Next, the three steps to transforming your mindset will be covered: controlling your thoughts, retraining your thoughts, and guarding your mind.

Control Your Thoughts

As we have previously discussed, our thoughts lead to actions. *"For as he thinketh within himself, so is he..."* (Psalm 23:7a, ASV). "The mind is the forerunner of all actions" (Meyer, 2011, p. 3). Our actions are a direct result of our thoughts, which can be influenced by whatever we allow into our ear gates and eye gates, as we attempt to emulate something or someone that appeals to us. Whether we admit it verbally or not, we pattern our lives or portions thereof after the lives of others. If we are influenced by factors that will benefit us positively, we will reap positive results. Otherwise, we can find ourselves travelling down a rabbit hole of despair, anguish, pain, and regret.

"For those who are according to the flesh and are controlled by its unholy desires set their minds on and pursue those things which gratify the flesh, but those who are according to the Spirit and are controlled by the desires of the Spirit set their minds on and seek those things which gratify the [Holy] Spirit."

Romans 8:5 (AMPC)

For most of us, our life-altering choices began in adolescence and developed into patterns we unwittingly committed on into adulthood. "Satan begins to initiate his well-laid plans and to sow his deliberate deception at a very young age" (Meyer, 2011, p. 10). To combat and undo Satan's influence and to initiate different actions and reactions than the ones we have been accustomed to producing, we need to change our thoughts. "Positive minds produce positive lives. Negative minds produce negative lives. Positive thoughts are always full of faith and hope. Negative thoughts are always full of fear and doubt" (Meyer, 2011, p. 37).

"It shall be done for you as you have believed."

Matthew 8:13b (NASB)

Matthew 8:5-13 describes Jesus' response to the request of a Roman centurion in Capernaum. The Gentile officer has a servant who is paralyzed and suffering greatly. The centurion says Jesus does not need to come to his home, but He can heal the man with a word. As a man with authority, the soldier recognizes Jesus' right to command, even with respect to healing. Jesus applauds the centurion's faith and tells him his servant has been healed.

When Jesus told the centurion it would be done as he had believed, He was not telling him that his faith is the power ultimately responsible for the work of healing. Jesus was telling him what he believed Jesus could do had been done. In other words, Jesus could have healed the servant whether the centurion believed it or not, but his faith in Jesus proved true, resulting in the instant healing of his servant.

Via this verse, Jesus is also informing us that whatever we believe to be true can be done for us. Again, what we hold true in our hearts is what will manifest in our lives. Whether the ideas were planted from something we witnessed firsthand, overheard, or read somewhere, we internalized the ideas, and they became our truth. Nevertheless, if we have a heart and mind to change our thought patterns, we will see change in our lives overtime.

Read the following three reasons to help you understand why you must manage your thoughts to effectuate different outcomes in your life.

1. Manage your mind because your thoughts control your life. Proverbs 4:23(GNT) says, *"Be careful how you think [for] your life is shaped by your thoughts."* Your thoughts have tremendous ability to shape your life for good or for bad. For example, maybe you accepted the thought someone told you when you were growing up or in a relationship: "You're worthless. You don't matter." If you accepted that thought, even though it was wrong, it shaped your life.

Notice this- Words have the power to alter the course of a person's life regardless of whether or not the words are factual. Furthermore, the receiver/ hearer of the words has the authority to either accept or reject the words. Personally, when I am in agreement with someone's words that have been spoken into my life, I will say, "I receive that," or "I'm in full agreement." In contrast, if I do not agree with the words, I will respond by saying, "I reject that," or "Do not speak that into my life." Also, it is important to note that regardless of what you verbalize aloud, if you mentally internalize the person's words as truth, the words can impact your life. Voicing your concern today is taking the power into your own hands.

The good news though is your life can be reshaped if you accepted the words then later reject them after they took root. That is what the transformation is all about. *BUT*, you must be willing to undergo the transformation, which will require you to be steadfast in your objective. Otherwise, the time and attention given to the matter will be futile if not seen through to the end.

2. Manage your mind because the mind is the battleground for sin. All temptation happens in the mind. Paul says in Romans 7:22-23 (TLB), *"I love to do God's will so far as my new nature is concerned; but there is something else deep within me, in my lower nature, that is at war with my mind and wins the fight and makes me a slave to the sin that is still within me. In my mind I want to be God's willing servant, but instead I find myself still enslaved to sin."*

Contrary to popular belief, even those who possess a tremendous love for God still possess a propensity to sin. That propensity is overcome by the person's mindset. Unlike many believers today, Apostle Paul was not afraid to admit the truth. Facing the truth is what allows one to be free. Proverbs 24:16 informs us, *"For though a righteous man may fall seven times, he still gets up; but the wicked stumble in bad times."*

Not only is the mind the battleground where the seeds of sin are planted, but it is also the place where Satan can plant his lies and allow them to grow and take root, unless the person interrupts his plan of destruction. Once a false belief takes root or a negativity springs up, the devil can do with it as he pleases, usually causing someone's life to be headed down a destructive path. Remember, regardless of Satan's temptations, you can withstand his wiles (Ephesians 6:11). You can resist Satan, and he will flee (James 4:7).

Pastor Joyce Meyer shared her personal experience with her own mindset in her revised version of *Battlefield of the Mind* (2011). She stated, "For most of my life, I didn't think about what I was thinking about. I simply thought whatever fell into my head. I had no revelation that Satan could inject thoughts into my mind. Much of what was in my head was either lies that Satan was telling me or just plain nonsense- things that really were not worth spending my time thinking about. The devil was controlling my life because he was controlling my thoughts" (p. 57).

3. Manage your mind because it is the key to peace and happiness. An unmanaged mind leads to tension; a managed mind leads to tranquility. An unmanaged mind leads to conflict; a managed mind leads to confidence. When you do not try to control your mind and the way you direct your thoughts, you will have an enormous amount of stress in your life. But a managed mind leads to strength, security, and serenity.

Have you ever noticed some people are always negative while other people are usually upbeat and positive? Imagine what must be going through the minds of those who are negative. For negative thoughts to flow freely from their lips like molten lava, negative thoughts must be permeating their mind space. And, for those who constantly speak positivity and are filled with cheer, peace, joy, and happiness, their minds must be filled with those types of thoughts. What we spend time focusing on and thinking about will manifest in our lives.

"You should take inventory on a regular basis and ask yourself, 'What have I been thinking about?' Spend some time examining your thought life" (Meyer, 2011, p. 61). The examination process is worth the time you put into it.

Managing your thoughts as the first step on the pathway to transforming your mind is what we are admonished to do by Apostle Paul in Romans 12:2. According to *Ellicott's Commentary for English Readers* (1979),

> It is the difference between an outward conformity or disguise and a thorough inward assimilation. The Christian is not to copy the fleeting fashions of the present time, but to be wholly transfigured in view of that higher mode of existence, in strict accordance with God's will, that he has chosen.
>
> 'To be conformed to this world' is to act as other men do, heathen who know not God; in opposition to this the Apostle exhorts his readers to undergo that total change which will bring them more into accordance with the will of God.
>
> 'The mind' (the mental faculties, reason, or understanding) is in itself neutral. When informed by an evil principle, it becomes an instrument of evil; when informed by the Spirit, it is an instrument of good. It performs the process of discrimination between good and evil.
>
> Prove. - As elsewhere, "discriminate, and so approve." The double process is included: first, of deciding what the will of God is; and, secondly, of choosing and acting upon it.

It involves an inward 'renewing of the mind' is regarded as the necessary antecedent of transformation of outward life.

According to *MacLaren's Expositions of Holy Scripture* (1959), Apostle Paul was explaining:

The life is to be transfigured, yet it remains the same, not only in the consciousness of personal identity, but in the main trend and drift of the character. There is nothing in the Gospel of Jesus Christ which is meant to obliterate the lines of the strongly marked individuality which each of us receives by nature. Rather the Gospel is meant to heighten and deepen these, and to make each man more intensely himself, more thoroughly individual and unlike anybody else. The perfection of our nature is found in the pursuit, to the furthest point, of the characteristics of our nature, and so, by reason of diversity, there is the greater harmony, and, all taken together, will reflect less inadequately the infinite glories of which they are all partakers. But whilst the individuality remains, and ought to be heightened by Christian consecration, yet a change should pass over our lives, like the change that passes over the winter landscape when the summer sun draws out the green leaves from the hard black boughs, and flashes a fresh colour over all the brown pastures. There should be such a change as when a drop or two of ruby wine falls into a cup, and so diffuses a gradual warmth of tint over all the whiteness of the water. Christ in us, if we are true to Him, will make us more ourselves, and yet new creatures in Christ Jesus.

And the transformation is to be into His likeness who is the pattern of all perfection. We must be moulded after the same type. There are two types possible for us: this world; Jesus Christ. We have to make our choice which is to be the headline after which we are to try to write. 'They that make them are like unto them.' Men resemble their gods; men become more or less like their idols. What you conceive to be desirable you will more and more assimilate yourselves to. Christ is the Christian man's pattern; is He not better than the blind, corrupt world?

That transformation is no sudden thing, though the revolution which underlies it may be instantaneous. The working *out* of the new motives, the working *in* of the new power, is no mere work of a moment. It is a lifelong task till the lump be leavened. Michael Angelo, in his mystical way, used to say that sculpture effected its aim by the removal of parts; as if the statue lay somehow hid in the marble block. We have, day by day, to work at the task of removing the superfluities that mask its outlines. Sometimes with a heavy mallet, and a hard blow, and a broad chisel, we have to take away huge masses; sometimes, with fine tools and delicate touches, to remove a grain or two of powdered dust from the sparkling block, but always to seek more and more, by slow, patient toil, to conform ourselves to that serene type of all perfectness that we have learned to love in Jesus Christ.

And remember, brethren, this transformation is no magic change effected whilst men sleep. It is a commandment which we have to brace ourselves to perform, day by day to set ourselves to the task of more completely assimilating ourselves to our Lord. It comes to be a solemn question for each of us whether we can say, 'Today I am liker Jesus Christ than I was yesterday; today the truth which renews the mind has a deeper hold upon me than it ever had before.'

But this positive commandment is only one side of the transfiguration that is to be affected. It is clear enough that if a new likeness is being stamped upon a man, the process may be looked at from the other side; and that in proportion as we become liker Jesus Christ, we shall become more unlike the old type to which we were previously conformed. And so, says Paul, 'Be not conformed to this world, but be ye transformed.' He does not mean to say that the nonconformity precedes the transformation. They are two sides of one process; both arising from the renewing of the mind within.

Two additional Bible verses regarding the mind and the commentary that follows will provide additional insight on the importance of transforming your mind.

"Casting down imaginations, and every high thing that exalteth itself against the knowledge of God, and bringing into captivity every thought to the obedience of Christ."

II Corinthians 10:5 (KJV)

Gill's Exposition of the Entire Bible (1748-63) provides the following the commentary:

> Imaginations are "the carnal reasonings of the minds of natural men against God, his providences and purposes, against Christ, and the methods of salvation, and every truth of the Gospel; which are all disproved, silenced, and confounded by the preaching of the word, which though reckoned the foolishness and weakness of God, appears to be wiser and stronger than

men; and whereby the wisdom of the wise is destroyed, and the understanding of the prudent brought to nothing."

The things that exalt themselves against God are "every proud thought of the heart, every great swelling word of vanity, every big look, even all the lofty looks and haughtiness of men, with every airy flight, and high towering imagination, reasoning, and argument advanced against the Gospel of Christ.

To bring into captivity every thought is to, "illustrate it with divine light, that it clearly sees Christ to be the alone, able, willing, full, and suitable Savior and a king; such an enlightened soul looks to him alone for life and salvation, ventures on him, and relies upon him, and is desirous and willing to be saved by him in his own way; he receives and embraces all his truths and doctrines with faith and love, and obeys them from the heart, and cheerfully and willingly submits to all his commands and ordinances; for though he is taken by the grace of God, and his strongholds, reasonings, and high thoughts are demolished by the power of God in the Gospel, and he himself is carried captive, yet not against, but with his will, to be a voluntary subject of Christ, and cheerfully to submit to the sceptre of his kingdom.

"Listen to counsel and receive instruction, That you may be wise in your latter days. There are many plans in a man's heart, Nevertheless the Lord's counsel - that will stand."

Proverbs 19:20-21 (NKJV)

Gill's Exposition of the Entire Bible (1748-63) provides the following commentary:

> Hear counsel, and receive instruction... of parents, masters, and ministers; especially the counsel and instruction of Wisdom, of Jesus Christ, the Wisdom of God, the wonderful Counsellor, and of his Gospel and of the Scriptures, which are able to make a man wise unto salvation; in the latter end of life, at death; that then it may appear a man has been so wise as to be concerned for a future state, for the good of his soul in another world; by listening to the counsel and instruction of Christ, in his word, by looking to him, and believing in him, for life and salvation. There are many devices in a man's heart... some about civil things; to get wealth and riches: to obtain honour and glory among men; to attain to a long life, and to perpetuate their memories after death: some

about sinful things; to gratify their carnal lusts and sensual appetites; and to do mischief to others, particularly the people of God, and the cause and interest of Christ; nevertheless, the counsel of the Lord, that shall stand; and can never be frustrated by the devices of man's heart; though there are many."

Retrain Your Thoughts

To assist in your personal transformation within your mental space, there are several activities you can engage in to initiate the process. One method for doing so is by substituting positive thoughts for negative ones.

Here is an exercise that can assist you. Over the next few days, focus on the negative thoughts that consistently infiltrate your mind. To complete this exercise, you can use the sample that follows on page 113, or you can take a sheet of lined paper and fold it in half vertically, creating two columns. On the left side of the page (in the first column), list each negative thought. Then, use the right side of the page (the second column) to write a positive affirmation that corresponds to the negative thought, which should be in direct opposition to it.

Use as many sheets as necessary. Keep the list(s) handy. Each time one of the negative thoughts surfaces, read the positive affirmation aloud. Please note- Using this activity to replace negative, cancerous thoughts "is not to suggest we should not learn from our past mistakes or plan our future intelligently. The only thing is we should stop [running the thoughts] over and over [through our mind] once we have learned from our past and decided about our future" (Rishi, 2023).

Negative Thoughts	Positive Affirmation
________________	________________
________________	________________
________________	________________
________________	________________
________________	________________
________________	________________
________________	________________
________________	________________
________________	________________
________________	________________
________________	________________
________________	________________
________________	________________
________________	________________
________________	________________
________________	________________
________________	________________
________________	________________

Eventually, if you practice the positive affirmations, they will begin to take root in your life. Proverbs 18:21a (BSB) says, *"Life and death are in the power of the tongue."* Whatever you practice telling yourself will germinate (take root) and begin to produce fruit in your life. What type of fruit do you want? Healthy fruit or poisonous fruit? The key here is thinking and speaking in agreement with God's will and plan for your life (Meyer, 2011).

A second method to change your thoughts is instead of re-playing old conversations over and over again in your mind, confront those thoughts. What you think about is *your* choice, and you do not have to believe every thought you have. When you confront a thought that you know is not true, you can choose to change what you are thinking! A positive change in your thoughts will lead to a healthy change in your emotional state and a positive change in your actions.

Pastor Meyer stated, "I realized at that time most of my life had been made miserable by evil thoughts and forebodings. Yes, I had circumstances that were very difficult, but even when I didn't, I was still miserable because my thoughts were poisoning my outlook and robbing me of [the] ability to enjoy life and see good days. Even if nothing bad was happening at the time, I always vaguely sensed that something bad was about to happen. Because of that I was unable to really enjoy my life" (p. 45).

Changing an active thought that is playing in your mind is as easy as changing the channel on a television. If you are browsing channels to find a good movie, when you come to the first channel, you stop, view for a minute or two, and decide whether to continue watching or to move on. Entertaining thoughts can be decided upon in the same manner. When a thought comes to mind, if it is displeasing, do not harp on it. Change the thought. Yes, it can be difficult. However, it is not impossible. You can even aide the shift in your thinking by picking up a book to read, turning on music, or yes, even turning on a good movie. A good, positive distraction will work every time, and eventually, the thought will surface less and less frequently.

"For he that will love life, and see good days [good- whether apparent or not], let him refrain his tongue from evil, and his lips that they speak no guile [treachery, deceit]."

I Peter 3:10 (KJV)

A third way to retrain your thoughts is by counting your blessings. Realizing how blessed you truly are can assist in transforming your current outlook. Many times, we may find ourselves believing our life is going nowhere or is not where we would like it to be. However, if we examine the totality of our lives, we may find our life is pretty good despite some pitfalls we may have suffered. If we focus on one or a few bad incidents we have endured in our life, we can become overwhelmed by those situations and lose focus on our life as a whole.

"Gratitude unlocks the fullness of life. It turns what we have into enough, and more. It turns denial into acceptance, chaos to order, confusion to clarity. It can turn a meal into a feast, a house into a home, a stranger into a friend."

Melody Beattie

When you feel yourself being overwhelmed by an unfortunate incident or season in your life, shift your focus to the positive moments or achievements you have fulfilled in your life. Similar to the first activity, you may desire to make a list of your accomplishments or happy seasons of your life. Some people have an ego wall, not to lift themselves up in pride, but to remind themselves of their proudest moments.

An ego wall is one where people place awards, certificates, degrees, plagues, and even photos and quotes to encourage them and remind them of days past. Remembering days past can and will inspire us for days and seasons that lie ahead.

"There are two things to aim at in life: first, to get what you want; and after that, to enjoy it. Only the wisest of mankind achieve the second."

Logan Pearsall Smith

"A great way to change your thoughts is to appreciate and enjoy what you already have. [This is truly the essence of counting your blessings.] This is not to suggest that you should not aspire for a[n even] better life. Enjoy whatever amount of success you have achieved instead of feeling sad about what you have not been able to achieve. There is nothing wrong with always [setting] higher benchmarks or goals, but failure to reach them should not spoil your enjoyment of what you already have" (Rishi, 2023).

"If you realize that you have enough, you are truly rich."

Lao Tzu

Guard Your Mind

The third requirement to successfully undergo a mental transformation is to guard your mind. Believers are forewarned throughout the Bible to guard their hearts and minds against all wickedness and unfruitful information. One such warning can be found in Proverbs 4:23 (KJV), which states, *"Above all else, guard your heart for everything you do flows from it."* What we indulge in can contaminate our heart and our minds, affecting what flows from them.

To successfully transform your mind, you must guard it at all costs. Not only must you rid your mind of the present contamination, but you must ensure it is not re-contaminated. Philippians 4:6-7 (KJV) provides a method for protecting our heart and mind: *"Be careful for nothing; but in everything by prayer and supplication with thanksgiving let your requests be made known unto God. And the peace of God which passeth all understanding shall keep your hearts and minds through Christ Jesus."* The peace that comes as a bi-product of our relationship with God will keep our mind and heart focused on Him.

If we fail to put safeguards in place, we will be much more susceptible to the schemes of the enemy, which come to weaken us in our strongest yet most vulnerable area: our mind. Romans 7:23 (ESV) offers a bit of wisdom when Apostle Paul wrote, *"But I see in my members another law waging war against the law of my mind and making me captive to the law of sin that dwells in my members."*

If we are going to guard our mind, we must first ensure we are in the proper frame of mind prior to doing so. It may not be an easy process, but it is a process we must be willing to undertake. Over-hauling our thoughts is necessary. Then, retraining our thoughts follows. After completing both steps by use of some of the methods mentioned earlier, you will be ready to guard your mind.

There are many methods you can use to guard your heart. The following three methods will prove useful. First, examine your current relationships. As you survey each relationship (platonic, familial, and erotic) ask yourself the following questions.

1. Who do you engage with on a regular basis?
2. How much influence does that person hold in your life?
3. Is the interaction positive for you and producing good fruit?

4. How are your emotions before, during, and after engaging with the person?
5. Is the person contributing beneficially to your life?
6. Does your engagement cause you to have unhealthy thoughts or produce actions that are harmful to you?
7. How are your sleep patterns as they relate to your interaction with the individual?

After you answer each question for each individual, you will need to decide if you can, should, and will continue your relationship with that individual at the same level of intensity as it is currently. That is the second method in guarding your heart: shifting or ending relationships as needed. If your responses to the seven questions demonstrate unhealthy relationships, for your own security and to provide a positive outlook for your future narrative, you must decide whether or not it would be a wise choice to remain in the same type of relationship with that individual. Some of the relationships will need to be extinguished, while others can be shifted or remain the same.

For example, if you have a friend who does not offer any benefits in the relationship and the Lord has not mandated your involvement with the person and all you feel is stress and more stress, maybe even tension, then you need to eliminate that relationship from your life. You will be doing yourself and that person a favor.

On the other hand, maybe there is a person who is related to you and you cannot simply walk away. In that instance, you can reduce or limit your interaction with the person. Only interact when necessary and reduce the amount of time in order to reduce the amount of toxicity you are receiving from the individual.

The third method to guard your heart is to cultivate new relationships that are positive, healthy, and uplifting and will contribute to your growth. When looking to establish new, healthy relationships or friendships, use the follow guidelines.

1. When meeting someone new or re-connecting with an old friend with whom you have been out of touch, take your time and allow the relationship to develop at an unhurried pace. Moving too quickly can cause an emotional attachment to develop too quickly, while causing red flags to go ignored or unnoticed. Once an emotional attachment has been forged, breaking away from the person can be difficult.
2. Listen intently when the person speaks. What is important to the person? What does he/she spend the most time talking about? Does your interest align with his/hers?

3. As you learn more about the person, answer these questions:
    a) What is the person's temperament?
    b) What types of problems is the person currently facing?
    c) What interest does the person have in you?
4. Are there any red flags that are popping up for you, giving you pause about engaging with this person? Trust your instincts.
5. Invite the person out for lunch to see how your one-on-one time goes. Afterward, assess if the time spent together was pleasant or uncomfortable.

These questions are just a few that you should ask yourself in an attempt to ensure you are not inviting someone into your life that will add toxicity. Life has enough problems of its own, and we do not want to add to our stress level by taking on unneeded problems.

The four method is guarding your eye and ear gates, which means only listen to and watch that which is beneficial to your personal growth. In doing so, you will learn how to weed out negativity rather than absorb it as you did before.

I am sure you have a question right now: What about entertainment? Entertainment is wonderful and offers many benefits, such as laughter, happiness, rest for the mind, a reprieve from the day-to-day problems that are not going away, etc. However, be careful what you choose as your entertainment. Some items, shows, games, etc. may entertain but can be harmful in that they may lead to negative behavior patterns and habits. Choose wisely!

Here is a closing thought about transforming your mind: Pastor Joyce Meyer (2011) asserts, "Many [people] want [a better] life, but they are passively sitting around wishing that something good would happen to them. Often, they are jealous of others who are living [a peaceful, healthy existence] and are resentful that their own lives are so difficult. If you desire victory over your problems, if you truly want to live [a better life], *you must have a backbone and not just a wishbone!* You must be active – not passive. Right action begins with right thinking. Don't be passive in your mind. Start today choosing right thoughts" (p. 147).

Transforming your mindset may not be an easy task, but if you follow the step-by-step methods presented in this chapter and remain diligent, you will see the transformation take place very soon.

KEEP YOUR **THOUGHTS** POSITIVE
BECAUSE YOUR THOUGHTS BECOME
YOUR **WORDS**.
KEEP YOUR **WORDS** POSITIVE
BECAUSE YOUR WORDS BECOME
YOUR **BEHAVIOR**.
KEEP YOUR **BEHAVIOR** POSITIVE
BECAUSE YOUR BEHAVIOR BECOMES
YOUR **HABITS**.
KEEP YOUR **HABITS** POSITIVE BECAUSE
YOUR HABITS BECOME YOUR **VALUES**.
KEEP YOUR **VALUES** POSITIVE BECAUSE
YOUR VALUES BECOME YOUR **DESTINY**.

Mahatma Gandhi

CHAPTER FOUR

Transform Your Will

Chapter Four
Transform Your Will

"Among these we as well as you once lived and conducted ourselves in the passions of our flesh [our behavior governed by our corrupt and sensual nature], obeying the impulses of the flesh and the thoughts of the mind."

Ephesians 2:3 (AMPC)

In Ephesians 2:3, Apostle Paul provides a warning against governing our lives by the impulses of our mind and our flesh, by the thoughts of our carnal mind. We can also apply this warning to living according to the dictates of our past experiences and patterns. "What we think of as our 'patterns' –at some point they were necessary adaptations for us or at least are built on assumptions about how the world works. While they might seem irrational, [they] are actually drawn from real experience with the world" (Olds, 2023).

Living according to past experiences and patterns can cause you to live an unproductive life where situations transpire in an unstructured and unplanned manner. "What was adaptive in the past, may be maladaptive for your present life. When your brain is learning these patterns and figuring out what to expect and how to respond to life [as an adolescent or young adult], that world differs in important ways from the world at large. Or, perhaps that original world [when you were younger], those original data points, simply differ from your life now [as a functioning adult]" (Olds, 2023). Furthermore, living life according to an ungoverned will can prove unfruitful and unproductive as it relates to accomplishing obtainable, fruit-producing goals.

I am reminded of a simple yet powerful verse: Habakkuk 2:2, which instructs us to write the vision and make it plain. When you meditate and plan your life, rather than allowing life to just happen as it will, you will have a better outcome. Having a plan of action for your life is a portion of what is required to transform your will from doing whatever pops into your mind versus acting out the actions that are part of your life plan. If you find your life is not the way you imagined, it is because the thoughts you were thinking led to the actions you performed, and the actions led to the results you obtained, which many not align with the ones you desire, if you had actually given them prior thought.

In Psalm 143:4-5 (ESV), David shares, *"Therefore my spirit faints within me; my heart within me is appalled. I remember the days of old; I meditate on all that you have done; I ponder the work of your hands."* From these verses, we ascertain David's decision to <u>not</u> respond to the feelings of despair (he mentions in verse four with) meditation and prolonged pondering on his present condition. Rather, he elected to shift his focus from his present thoughts to entertain thoughts that were more pleasant (verse five). He understood if he meditated on his thoughts of gloom (verse four), he would internalize those feelings and doing so would result in unhealthy actions. However, training his thoughts on pleasant topics (verse five) would lead him to performing positive actions. Healthy thoughts lead to healthy life-sustaining actions.

Oftentimes, people doubt they can change the outlook of their life, and as a result, they opt to maintain the status quo of their dead-end job, their abusive relationship, and their overall unfulfilled life. Read the following biblical account of Apostle Peter, and witness how his change in perspective offered him a different outcome in his life.

> ***But the boat was by this time out on the sea, many furlongs distant from the land, beaten and tossed by the waves, for the wind was against them.***

And in the fourth watch of the night, Jesus came to them, walking on the sea.
And when the disciples saw Him walking on the sea, they were terrified and said, It is a ghost! And they screamed out with fright.
But instantly He spoke to them, saying, Take courage! I AM! Stop being afraid! And Peter answered Him, Lord, if it is You, command me to come to You on the water.
He said, Come! So Peter got out of the boat and walked on the water, and he came toward Jesus.
But when he perceived and felt the strong wind, he was frightened, and as he began to sink, he cried out, Lord, save me!
Instantly Jesus reached out His hand and caught and held him, saying to him, O you of little faith, why did you doubt?
And when they got into the boat, the wind ceased.

Matthew 14:24-32 (AMPC)

This set of verses serve as a good example of faith- believing the unbelievable. You can transform your narrative by having faith, understanding the power of your will, having guidelines in place for accomplishing goals, and training your focus. If you spend too much time focusing on a circumstance, you will take the attention off the goal. If your objective is to transform your will, your actions, and your responses to the stimuli around you, you must shift your focus, strengthen your faith, and change the way you view obstacles.

Peter doubted he could continue to walk on the water, even when he was already doing it. This example demonstrates how important it is to have faith and stay focused on the task at hand. We cannot allow our feelings, comments from others, or distractions to get us off course of attaining a goal.

Remember, our will is demonstrated via our actions. Once our mind is set upon something, we act it out in our body. Sometimes, our actions yield favorable results. Other times, our actions yield undesirable results. Oftentimes, the undesired results come from learned behavior, either modeled before us or either serve as a response to an unwanted action from someone else.

Read the following example about Robert to see how our behavior can yield undesirable results.

> Robert was physically bullied in his youth, and he reacted by shouting expletives at his attackers because he was unable to physically fight back. The practice of cursing eventually became habitual and was one that lasted for years. Later in life, when Robert again faced situations that frustrated him, like the incidents

of bullying did, he responded in the same manner- by cursing his supposed attackers.

Unfortunately, Robert's short temper and foul language caused him to lose a few jobs, leaving him without income to properly take care of his basic needs for months on end. Learning that his behavior was the direct cause of a personal situation he had experienced in his youth, Robert began to understand he could not continue along the same trajectory due to the yielded unfavorable results.

Now, Robert wants to alter his behavior in an effort to produce more favorable results. After flying off the handle for years in an attempt to protect himself, Robert now wants better for himself as well as for those with whom he comes in contact. Although he really had no desire to cause harm to those around him, it was an inevitable bi-product of his learned response to unfavorable conditions.

Robert attempted to shift his behavior from the destructive pattern he had formed to patterns that are more beneficial. He had difficulty with the shift even though he had a sincere desire to change.

Why is it difficult to change behavior?

First, I must inform you that the problem is not with the brain, for the brain is adaptive to different situations a person may encounter. So, then the question becomes, "If the brain is so malleable, what causes the process of change to be difficult?" "You may be wondering, if my brain is so great at adapting, why doesn't it just continue to adapt? [Why doesn't it] continue to learn and make new assumptions and make new behavioral patterns that actually fit what is in front of me now? Well, here's the rub: our brain if left to its own devices doesn't actively update its view of reality. Once the brain feels that it knows something, either through a million repetitions of experience or one big powerful experience (which we would call a trauma), it doesn't just always stay open for continued input" (Olds, 2023).

Most of our behavior has become automatic. When repeated over time, those behaviors become habitual. A good example of this is driving. When you first learn to drive, it requires conscious effort to learn and remember all the right steps: using all the mirrors, signaling, maneuvering, etc. But as time goes on, those actions form habits. This happens when you have practiced them so often that they become automatic. As such, successful behavioral change can be difficult because our brain has been programmed to function in fixed patterns.

However, the same mechanism that trains our problem behavior as mental habits is often the solution to changing them (Eatough, 2021).

Our brains must undergo the process of neuroplasticity, which is the process by which our brains change as we learn. It refers to the physical structures of the brain. Every time you learn something new, a new connection forms in your brain. The newly formed connection is weak at first, but with repetition, the connection becomes stronger over time. This process causes the new, healthier behavior to become a habit (Eatough, 2021).

The three stages of the neuroplastic change process are:

- **Chemical change:** these are short-term changes in brain chemistry in response to new behavior. They boost short-term memory and improve motor skills short term.
- **Structural change**: new connections form, altering the brain's structure. This boosts long-term memory and long-term improvement of motor skills.
- **Functional change**: entire brain networks change, becoming more efficient in their functioning. This is when lasting behavioral change occurs.

(Eatough, 2021).

So, to break and rid yourself of old habits, strong neural connections must be weakened. Simultaneously, the old habits are replaced with positive long-lasting behaviors that are being strengthened. However, this process can prove difficult as setbacks arise. Setbacks can easily knock us back into our old mental patterns and behaviors. Therefore, it is imperative to exercise a strong will to bring the desired changes to fruition (Eatough, 2021).

Before you start your planned stages of change, you must first understand the elements of change. These are the factors that will either assist or hinder you in achieving your desired behavior change(s). Behavioral Science Change Theory proposes different models, and each includes different elements of change. For simplicity, we can break them down into four main ones (Eatough, 2021).

1. Your willingness to change

How ready are you to change your current behavior? Are you changing for yourself or someone else? Self-motivation is a key factor in causing your new behavior to become permanent. If you desire change for personal growth and/or improvement rather than changing as the result of the prompting of another person, the changes are more apt to be permanent.

2. The benefits of change

Awareness of the benefits of your target behavior will help you stay motivated. It will also increase your resilience and ability to overcome setbacks.

3. Your barriers to change

Are your current circumstances preventing you from changing? Identify any barriers to behavior change and list any possible solutions. For example, if one of the changes you desire to make is a change in your temperament and you are involved with volatile situations, you may want to remove yourself from the situations as part of the process if possible.

4. The likelihood of relapse

When you begin your journey to make lasting changes, you will face obstacles and setbacks along the way. Being aware of possible challenges will help you prepare for and overcome them. This simply means you must be realistic about the difficulty of change while understanding your willingness and open-mindedness are key assets to achieving your desired goal(s).

According to the Transtheoretical Model of Change, which was developed by Prochaska and DiClemente in the late '70s, there are six stages of behavior change (Eatough, 2021).

1. Precontemplation stage

At this stage, people are not yet aware of the negative behavior they need to change. They do not see their behavior as a problem and are not interested in getting help. They may become defensive if someone pressures them to change. They also avoid speaking, reading, or thinking about it. They may also absorb information about this problem from family, friends, or the media, but will not take action until they see it as being problematic.

2. Contemplation stage

At this stage, people are aware of the negative consequences or problems. But they are not yet ready to change their unhealthy behavior. They do start thinking about it, however. They know it is necessary to change but are not ready.

They might weigh the pros and cons and whether the long-term benefits outweigh the short-term effort. This stage can last a few days or an entire lifetime, depending on the individual.

3. Preparation or determination stage

This is the phase when a person is ready to make a change. They become committed to changing and motivated to take the necessary steps. They read, talk, and gather information about the problem. The preparation stage is crucial to the success of behavior change. Skipping this stage can drastically decrease one's chances of success.

4. Action stage

At this stage, people use the strategies they learned in the previous phase to start a new, healthy behavior. This takes willpower, and there is a high risk of failure and slipping back into the old behavior and habits. It can help to avoid external temptation and set rewards for achieving intermediate goals. The sup-port of others is also essential at this stage.

5. Maintenance stage

In this stage, people have made progress and have realized the benefits of changing. They realize maintaining change will require effort, but they are aware of its value. They create strategies to prevent relapse until the new habit becomes familiar and natural.

6. Relapse stage

This stage is when people slip back into their old behaviors and habits. Relapsing is a normal part of the process of change. The key is to identify the trigger that caused the failure and look for new and better strategies for dealing with it. Bearing in mind the benefits of the change help regain motivation when restarting the stages of change model.
(Eatough, 2021)

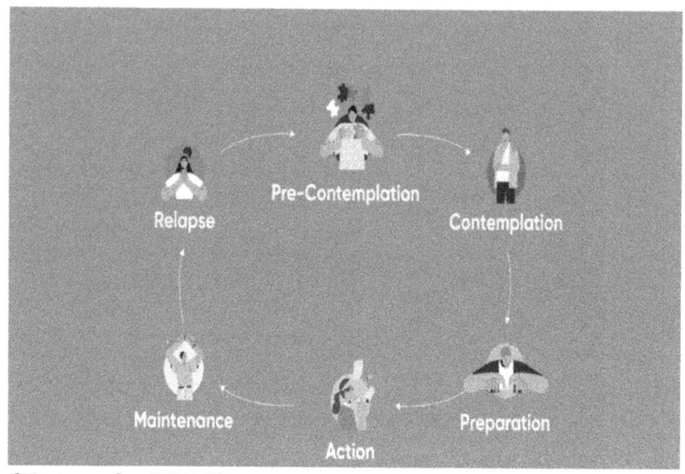

(Eatough, 2021)

Here are nine steps Robert can take to change his behavior. You too can benefit from following these steps if you have behaviors or reactions that lead to unfavorable results.

> *# 1: Recognize the action and commit to making a change.*
> It is important to identify the negative behavior to change it. If people are unaware of their own behavior, they are unlikely to change it. One way people can identify their own negative behaviors is self-reflection. Self-awareness and self-reflection are key steps in identifying and changing one's own negative behavior.

Look in the mirror and say it out loud: "Only I can stop ________." Then, vow to yourself to make a concerted effort to cease the actions.

 # 2: Analyze the reasons for your negative behavior

To understand the reasons for your negative behavior, a good step is to list the things that trigger you.

Some people behave negatively because they are stressed out and need a break from their work. Others might be having a bad day and venting their frustrations on others. Some people might feel low self-esteem and need validation from others.

 # 3: Pay closer attention to what you are doing.

So much of what we do each day is done without having given any pre-thought to the matter. If you consciously focus your thoughts on any actions you are about to take, you will have an increased chance of stopping the negative behavior.

 # 4: Slow down your thinking to focusing on your overall behavior.

When your mind starts racing, it is your first clue that you might be about to take an action you may later regret. Take a deep breath and choose a positive action instead.

 # 5: Identify situations, people, and events that trigger your negative behavior.

For example, perhaps in social situations, you talk too much. You interrupt others, finish their sentences, and other people have little opportunity to talk. Take an honest look within yourself and your annoying behavior. When is it most likely to happen?

 # 6: Decide what you will do instead.

We may not be able to change our old habits as easily as we would like, but we can replace them with new ones. If you want to start a new habit, you need to take it step by step. You can start by setting up a plan, and then work on it every day until it becomes a habit.

Keeping with the earlier example of talking too much, you could make the decision to "experiment" with listening to others, just to see what you can learn from them. You would talk less and practice listening each time you are in a social situation. Later, ask yourself, "How did I do? How did it feel to listen instead of talk?"

Who knows what great things could happen from making a decision to cease your troublesome behavior!

 # 7: Ask close friends and family members for their help in stopping the behavior.

For example, tell your sister that you are trying to stop interrupting people so much. Ask her to touch your elbow at the family reunion tomorrow each time she notices you interrupting. This way, you will have a cue to stop the behavior.

 # 8: Say you are sorry when you engage in the behavior if it affects others.

Staying with the example of talking too much, as soon as you realize you interrupted someone, say, "I'm sorry I interrupted you. Please do go on. I'm interested in what you were saying."

Showing humility will help you learn to stop the old behavior and change it to a more effective action.

 # 9: Seek expert guidance if you need it.

If you have been working on your troublesome actions for a while and have had less success than you want in stopping them,

asking a professional to assist you can be a big help.
(Garrett, 2022).

If seeking professional guidance is unafford-able, continue reading for another option that may be just as beneficial.

John C. Lilly, M.D. was a physician, neuro-physiologist, and pioneer of states of conscious-ness. He was a researcher with the National Institutes of Health and the Maryland Psychiatric Research Center. Lilly authored books exploring the depths of our consciousness (Brenner, 2013).

Lilly constructed a series of ordered questions meant to challenge held beliefs and to effectively change them. Ask yourself the questions and answer them, much as you would do with a therapist. Think of this exercise as a way to "self-dialogue" (Brenner, 2013).

Try this exercise. Choose any issue, attitude, behavior, or even bad habit you want to address and ask these questions.

- What are my goals when I engage in this behavior/way of thinking, feeling, believing, or acting? In other words, what am I getting out of doing it?

- By what means can I stop this behavior? What do I need to do in order to stop thinking, acting, behaving this way?

- What is my relationship with other people and the way I utilize that relationship that allows me to continue this behavior or to stop this behavior? This is a point often not considered. People that we hang out with may hold the same attitudes or beliefs, and there may be pressure from the group not to change.

- Am I capable of stopping this behavior? In other words, how do I know I can stop?

- What is my orientation, when I engage in this behavior or when I stop this behavior? Where is this behavior leading me in either case?

- What do I have to eliminate in order to stop this behavior? What behavior(s) and/or people do I need to let go in order to stop doing what I'm doing?

- What do I have to assimilate to stop this behavior? What must I absorb/adopt to change this conditioned behavior?

- What must I do to bring my impulses in line with stopping this behavior? How do I extinguish the impulses/desire that perpetuates the behavior? When the impulse arises can I delay gratification? Can I substitute another thought or action in place of the impulse?

- What are my needs when I engage in this behavior and when I stop this behavior? Do I really need this behavior or just want or like having it? What habitual activities that support this behavior must be eliminated?

- What are the other possibilities in relationship to this behavior? What positive behaviors can potentially replace old negative patterns of behavior?

- What is the form this behavior takes? Describe detail by detail how this behavior is carried out on an ongoing basis. Is this behavior really important to your being? (If this is hard using an issue of your own choosing to work with, then use the example of smoking and the desire and goal to quit. Step by step think about all of the activities centered around smoking, not just smoking itself - people you hang out with that smoke, leaving the office for smoking breaks, hours thinking about cigarettes, anxiety about running out of cigarettes, and on and on.)

- What is the substance of this behavior? What does this negative, limiting (and sometimes potentially dangerous) behavior/attitude/belief really have to do with who I am? (Brenner, 2013)

Hopefully, at this point, you have taken time to examine your actions and the thoughts that led to those actions. After surveying your actions, you should have drawn conclusions about whether or not continuing specific actions and relationships yield beneficial or detrimental results that may have led to stagnation as it relates to obtaining your desires.

Remember how God created you. He created you as a free-will agent, one who can choose right versus wrong, good versus evil, prosperity versus poverty; success versus failure; happiness and joy versus sadness and despair. You have the autonomy to govern yourself according to your moral compass dictated by God's Word or by the world's standards. Everything you do is a choice. And, the choice is yours. You must decide from this day forward how you will operate for the remaining days of your life.

Yes, it is true you cannot control the world around you, but you can control your reactions to the stimuli you experience. Remember, you cannot control other people, just as other people cannot control you- unless you willingly relinquish your will over to them.

As believers, who will one day stand at the Judgment Seat (the Bema Seat of God) and give an answer for all we have done while on earth, particularly our service to Him in His Kingdom, we must make wise, deliberate choices. Are you ready to respond to the Lord? Do you have a reply ready? If not, you have an opportunity to clear the slate (by asking for forgiveness of actions that were not representative of Him) and starting afresh.

Wise people who understand Psalm 90:12, which says, *"So teach us to number our days, that we may apply our hearts unto wisdom,"* apply it to their life in the hopes that they will use the final days or stages of their life wisely and in a manner that is pleasing to God. And, it is important to note that you are not left alone to choose the correct choices on a daily basis. No, God will be with you every step of the way, but we must consult Him. Otherwise, we will be left on our own to decide our next move. Then, we should be ready to accept any resulting consequences.

Proverbs 3:5-6 (KJV) says, *"Trust in the LORD with all thine heart; And lean not unto thine own understanding. In all thy ways acknowledge him, And he shall direct thy paths."* You may have noticed, God's Word provides our every need. We must read it, meditate on it, assimilate it into our hearts and our lifestyles, allowing it to transform us through and through.

Be mindful that transformation is a process. It will not happen overnight. As mentioned earlier, you may experience setbacks, like Peter did when he shifted his focus from Jesus to the storm that surrounded him. Storms will come. Challenges will come. Difficult situations will manifest. Tempers will rage. Words will be shouted and screamed. But, through it all, do not succumb to a lifestyle of chaos. Look for the good in life. Look for the peace and calm.

Dare to be a changemaker in your life and in the life of others as you transform destructive tendencies and behaviors into ones that are more beneficial to the life you desire for yourself. Just because the world around you is in an uproar does not mean you have to be.

Be the change you want to see in others. You just may be the domino at the beginning of a chain, ready to set off a chain reaction in others. Do not blend into the crowd. Stand out from it. Dare to be different. Dare to allow your light to shine, and the Lord will be with you every step of the way because the steps of a good man are ordered by the Lord (Psalm 37:23).

Here are two additional methods you can use to change your behavior, accomplishing better outcomes in your life.

1. "Stand erect and hold your head high in trying circumstances.
We often tend to feel demoralized in adverse conditions. We stop and feel low as if we are bending under their weight. This happens both literally and figuratively. You will, however, surely feel better if you try to lift your spirits and also your head like a person determined to take up the challenge. This is the best way to get out of depression. Try it" (Rishi, 2023).

2. "Allow yourself to be playful and childlike.
Children are known for their innocence and simplicity of mind. They soon forget their quarrels with their friends and start playing together once again. This is the reason that generally they are

always happy and smiling. Translated into the language of the adults, we should learn to forget and forgive" (Rishi, 2023).

"The great man is he who does not lose his child[like] heart."

Mencius, Book IV

The following verses and corresponding commentaries will assist you as you transform your will.

"This book of the law shall not depart out of thy mouth; but thou shalt meditate therein day and night, that thou mayest observe to do according to all that is written therein: for then thou shalt make thy way prosperous, and then thou shalt have good success."

Joshua 1:8 (KJV)

The *Benson Commentary on the Old and New Testaments* provides the following commentary:

> Thou shalt constantly read it, and upon occasion discourse of it, and the sentence which shall come out of thy month, shall in all things be given according to this rule. [God's Word must be] diligently study, and upon all occasions consider what is God's will and thy duty. The greatness of thy place and employments shall not hinder thee from this work, because this is the only rule of thy private actions and public administrations.

Matthew Poole's Commentary contributes the following:

> to understand the mind and law of God himself, and not blindly to follow what any other should advise him to.

"Thy word have I hid in mine heart, that I might not sin against thee."

Psalm 119:11 (KJV)

Matthew Henry's Concise Commentary provides the following commentary:

> God's word is treasure worth laying up, and there is no laying it up safe but in our hearts, that we may oppose God's precepts to the dominion

of sin, his promises to its allurements, and his threatenings to its violence. Let this be our plea with Him to teach us his statutes, that, being partakers of his holiness, we may also partake of his blessedness. And those whose hearts are fed with the bread of life, should with their lips feed many.

"The steps of a* good *man are ordered by the LORD: and he delighteth in his way."

Psalm 37:23 (KJV)

Barnes' Notes on the Bible commentates the following:

The word rendered "ordered" means to stand erect; to set up; to found; to adjust, fit, direct. The idea here is, that all which pertains to the journey of a good man through life is directed, ordered, fitted, or arranged by the Lord. That is, his course of life is under the divine guidance and control.

Gill's Exposition of the Entire Bible offers the following commentary:

> ...such a man as is blessed of the Lord; the steps which he takes in life are ordered by the Lord, both with respect to things temporal and spiritual: his good conduct is not of himself, it is a blessing of the Lord, who directs and keeps the feet of his saints, and inclines them to take such steps, and pursue such methods, which he succeeds and prospers.

CHAPTER FIVE

Transform Your Emotions

Chapter Five
Transform Your Emotions

"Keep your heart with all diligence, For out of it spring the issues of life."

Proverbs 4:23 (NKJV)

The final task you must perform to shift your narrative is to transform your emotional state to one that is healthier by learning how to manage your emotions. A healthy emotional state will allow for a fruitful and more productive outcome to your life as a whole. Similar to the connection between thoughts leading to actions and vice versa, thoughts also lead to emotions, emotions lead to thoughts and actions, and actions lead to emotions. Therefore, all three parts of the soul (mind, will, and emotions) are interconnected and truly cannot be separated.

Notice this- a person is not void of emotions when he/she performs an action or has a thought. Neither is a person void of thoughts when he/she experiences an emotion or performs an action. However, a person can decide not to respond with an action after having a thought or experiencing an emotion. That is where control comes in.

Examine the following chart to understand the interconnectedness between thoughts (*mind*), behaviors/actions (*will*), and *emotions*.

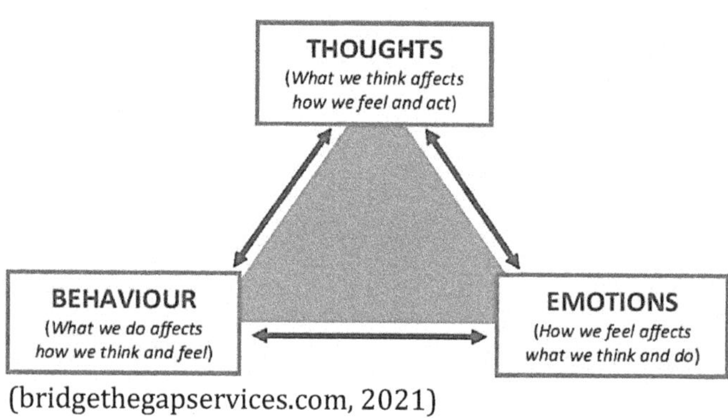

(bridgethegapservices.com, 2021)

Let's examine the chapter's opening verse from Proverbs 4:23: *"Keep your heart* [our emotions] *with all diligence, for out of it spring the issues of life."* King Solomon informs us here that the issues we experience in life are derived from that which is held within our heart. Now, I must clarify by saying, not all of our problems are a result of negative emotions we hold toward someone or something.

There are situations that result from the intentions and actions of others.

What King Solomon is pointing out though is the fact that we are responsible for the emotions and thoughts we hold within our hearts because they can lead to issues that cause problems within our life. Therefore, it is incumbent upon us to keep our hearts free from clutter (negativity).

To delve further into Proverbs 4:23, read the following commentary from *Gill's Exposition of the Entire Bible:*

> Keep thy heart with all diligence, The mind from vanity, the understanding from error, the will from perverseness, the conscience clear of guilt, the affections from being inordinate and set on evil objects, the thoughts from being employed on bad subjects; and the whole from falling into the hands of the enemy, or being the possession of Satan: great diligence had need be used in keeping it, since it is naturally so deceitful and treacherous; a strict eye is to be kept upon it; all the avenues to it to be watched, that nothing hurtful enters, or evil comes out; it is to be kept by all manner of means that can be thought of, by prayer, hearing, reading, meditation; and, above all, by applying to Christ for his grace and Spirit to sanctify, preserve, and keep it.
>
> It is the seat of natural life, from whence all actions of life are derived; it is, as philosophers

> say, the first that lives, and the last that dies; and it is the seat of spiritual life the principle of it is formed in it; from whence all spiritual and vital actions flow, and which lead unto and issue in eternal life: as is a man's heart, such is his state now, and will be hereafter; if the heart is quickened and sanctified by the grace of God, the man will live a life of faith and holiness here, and enjoy everlasting life hereafter.

Emotional health is an important part of your overall health. People who are emotionally healthy are in better control of their thoughts, feelings, and behaviors. They are able to cope with life's challenges to a better degree than those who struggle with other areas of their wellbeing. They tend to keep problems in perspective and bounce back from setbacks. They feel good about themselves and have good relationships with others (American Academy, 2020).

Being emotionally healthy does not mean you are happy all the time. It means you are aware of your emotions. You can deal with them, whether they are positive or negative. Emotionally healthy people still feel stress, anger, sadness, and a wide range of emotions. But they know how to manage their negative feelings. They can tell when a problem is more than they can handle on their own. They also know when to seek help from their doctor. Research shows that emotional health is a skill. There are steps you can take to improve your emotional health and be happier and whole (American Academy, 2020).

- **Be aware of your emotions and which reactions directly follow each emotion.**
  We all react differently to each emotion. For some, shedding tears follow sadness. For others, becoming quiet follows sadness. When you experience an emotion, take note of the response that follows. If your response is counter-productive, work to change your response. For example, if feelings of anger lead to destructive actions, such as destroying physical property, a new approach to dealing with anger must be instituted. For example, try counting to ten, giving yourself an opportunity to calm down before reacting. If that technique does not work, there are others you can try.
  1. Scream- to release the anxiety.
  2. Journal- write your feelings down.
  3. Do a workout routine to let off steam.
  4. Paint or illustrate- redirect your energy.
  5. Sing your favorite song.

6. Dance and release the stress.

- **Express your feelings in appropriate ways.**
  Let people close to you know when something is bothering you in a low, soft tone. Being transparent with others will let them know when to give you space or when you may need to talk things out. Keeping feelings of sadness or anger bottled inside adds to stress because you are attempting to cover up your true feelings, which can be stressful within itself. It can cause problems in your relationships and at work or school when others do not know what is going on inside you. Many times, we believe people should be able to read the exterior signs, but often other people miss the signs we believe are obvious. Verbal communication is so much better than causing people to play a guessing game with you.

- **Think before you act.**
  Give yourself time to think and be calm before you say or do something you might regret. Words cannot be rewound like a movie or deleted like an unsent

text message. Once they are released from your lips, they cannot be taken back. Feel free to refer back to the section titled *The Impact of Words* (on pages 76-84) for a more thorough explanation.

- **Manage stress.**
  Learn relaxation methods to cope with stress. These could include meditation, deep breathing, and exercise. Here is a list of techniques to manage stress:
  -Take deep breaths
  -Do a positive activity
  -Play sports
  -Think of something funny
  -Take a quick walk
  -Practice yoga
  -Stand up and stretch
  -Listen to music
  -Take a time out
  -Slowly count to ten
  -Use positive self-talk
  -Say something kind to yourself
  -Talk to a friend
  -Close your eyes and relax
  -Say, "I can do this."
  -Visualize your favorite place
  -Think of something happy
  -Think of a pet you love
  -Think about someone you love
  -Get enough sleep

-Eat a healthy snack
-Read a good book
-Jog in place
-Write in a journal
-Hum your favorite song
-Doodle on paper
-Draw a picture
-Color a coloring page
-Clean something
-Meditate
-Use a stress ball
-Dance
-Write a letter
-Look at pictures you've taken
-Make a gratitude list
-List your positive qualities
-Do something kind
-Give someone a hug
-Put a puzzle together
-Do something you love
-Build something
-Play with clay
-Hug a stuffed animal
-Rip paper into pieces
-Play an instrument
-Watch a good movie
-Take pictures
-Garden
-Write a list
-Keep a positive attitude
-Schedule time for yourself
-Blow bubbles
-Write a positive note
-Chew gum

-Paint your nails
-Write a story
-Blog
-Read a joke book
-Write a poem
-Drink cold water
-Draw cartoons
-Read a magazine
-Write a thank you note
-Count to 100
-Make a list for the future
-Read inspirational quotes
-Compliment yourself
-Visualize a stop sign
-Laugh
-Smile in the mirror
-Smile at others
-Look at animal pictures
-Hyperfocus on an object
-Notice 5 things you can see
-Paint with water colors
-Use a relaxation app
-Watch a funny video
-Drink some tea
-Cook or bake
-Plan a fun trip
-Use an I-statement
-Identify your emotions
-Express your feelings to someone
-Write down your thoughts
-Identify a positive thought
-Make your day's schedule
-List 10 positives about yourself
-Ask yourself, "What do I need right

now?"
-Tell someone you are thankful for them
-Pet an animal
-Make a list of choices
-Organize something
-Play a card game
-Listen to nature sounds
-Sit and relax all your muscles
-Ask for a break

- **Strive for balance.**
  Find a healthy balance between work and play and between activity and rest. Make time for things you enjoy that make you smile, feel good, and help you to take a load off. Take time to focus on positive things in your life. Please note, if you only attend to the required tasks in your life, such as work and study, which may be stress inducing, you will not schedule time to partake in activities that can contribute to stress release. For example, if your job is stressful and you work Monday-Friday from 8-5 and then go home and deal with a family and all the responsibilities that come with it and never take in a movie or engage in a calming activity during the week, your stress level will soar. As you are the

person who is ultimately responsible for your self-care, you are the one who controls your schedule. So, schedule calming and relaxing activities for yourself. They will greatly benefit your emotional health.

- **Connect with others.**
  Connecting with other people can assist in maintaining a healthy emotional balance. Between dealing with the natural stresses of life, taking time out to engage with others in less stressful situations can prove to be a healthy outlet. Think about the people you have a really good time with, ones who are emotionally healthy and are well balanced, i.e. those who are not full of drama. Make a lunch or dinner date. Plan a picnic in a beautiful, calm park or at the beach. Join a group of people who are going somewhere for an entertaining event, such as a concert or play. Say hello to a stranger, thereby brightening up their day and yours in the process. The positive connections you have with other people can be soothing.

- **Find purpose and meaning.**
  Oftentimes, feelings of worthlessness, distress, depression, anxiety, anger, and overwhelming stress arise when there is a lack of focus on something meaningful or of value. Take some time to figure out what is important to you in life, and focus on that. It could be your job, your family, volunteering, caregiving, or anything that defines your life, giving it meaning and purpose and more importantly, joy. Spend your time doing what feels meaningful to you.

- **Stay positive.**
  Considering the world in which we live, staying positive is not always an easy thing to do. Negativity surrounds us on a daily basis as the cancers of racism, discrimination on various levels, wars and threats of wars, marginalization, separatism, financial, educational, and housing inequities, and bigotry permeate our societies and the world at large. When we turn on the news, via the various platforms in which it avails itself, we allow the negativity to filter into our homes and ultimately into our spirits, via our ear gates and eye gates.

Regardless of where the negative stimuli exists (outside your home or workplace or inside), it is incumbent upon you to remain positive at all costs. Otherwise, your emotional health can be placed in jeopardy.

- **Take care of your physical health.** Exercise regularly, eat healthy meals, and get enough sleep. Do not abuse drugs or alcohol. Keep your physical health positive, so it does not negatively impact your emotional health.

The article titled "The Mental Health Benefits of Exercise," written by Lawrence Robinson, Jeanne Segal, Ph.D., and Melinda Smith, M.A. (2021) shares helpful tips regarding exercise and specific emotional disturbances a person may experience.

Exercise and Depression

"Studies show that exercise can treat mild to moderate depression as effectively as anti-depressant medication - but without the side-effects, of course. As one example, a recent study done by the Harvard T. H. Chan School of Public Health found that running for fifteen minutes a day or walking for an hour reduces the risk of major depression by 26%. In addition to relieving depression symptoms, research also shows that maintaining an exercise schedule can prevent you from relapsing [into depression].

Exercise is a powerful depression fighter for several reasons. Most importantly, it promotes all kinds of changes in the brain, including neural growth, reduced inflammation, and new activity patterns that promote feelings of calm and well-being. It also releases endorphins, powerful chemicals in your brain that energize your spirit and make you feel good. Finally, exercise can also serve as a distraction, allowing you to find some quiet time to break out of the cycle of negative thoughts that feed depression" (Robinson, Segal, & Smith, 2021).

Exercise and Anxiety

"Exercise is a natural and effective anti-anxiety treatment. It relieves tension and stress, boosts physical and mental energy, and enhances well-being through the release of endorphins. Anything that gets you moving can help, but you'll get a bigger benefit if you pay attention instead of zoning out.

Try to notice the sensation of your feet hitting the ground, for example, or the rhythm of your breathing, or the feeling of the wind on your skin. By adding this mindfulness element -really focusing on your body and how it feels as you exercise- you'll not only improve your physical condition faster, but you may also be able to interrupt the flow of constant worries running through your head" (Robinson, Segal, & Smith, 2021).

Exercise and Stress

"Ever noticed how your body feels when you're under stress? Your muscles may be tense, especially in your face, neck, and shoulders, leaving you with back or neck pain or painful headaches. You may feel a tightness in your chest, a pounding pulse, or muscle cramps. You may also experience problems, such as insomnia, heartburn, stomach ache, diarrhea, or frequent urination. The worry and discomfort of all these physical symptoms can in turn lead to even more stress, creating a vicious cycle between your mind and body.

Exercising is an effective way to break this cycle. As well as releasing endorphins in the brain, physical activity helps to relax the muscles and relieve tension in the body. Since the body and mind are so closely linked, when your body feels better so, too, will your mind" (Robinson, Segal, & Smith, 2021).

Exercise and ADHD

"Exercising regularly is one of the easiest and most effective ways to reduce the symptoms of ADHD and improve concentration, motivation, memory, and mood. Physical activity immediately boosts the brain's dopamine, norepinephrine, and serotonin levels - all of which affect focus and attention. In this way, exercise works in much the same way as ADHD medications, such as Ritalin and Adderall" (Robinson, Segal, & Smith, 2021).

Exercise and PTSD and Trauma

"Evidence suggests that by really focusing on your body and how it feels as you exercise, you can actually help your nervous system become 'unstuck' and begin to move out of the immobilization stress response that characterizes PTSD or trauma. Instead of allowing your mind to wander, pay close attention to the physical sensations in your joints and muscles, even your insides as your body moves. Exercises that involve cross movement and that engage both arms and legs - such as walking (especially in sand), running, swimming, weight training, or dancing - are some of your best choices.

Outdoor activities like hiking, sailing, rock climbing, mountain biking, whitewater rafting, and skiing (downhill and cross-country) have also been shown to reduce the symptoms of PTSD" (Robinson, Segal, & Smith, 2021).

Here are three tips suggested by Raj Rishi (2023) in "15 Powerful Ways to Transform Your Thoughts and Transform Your Life."

Seek happiness and contentment in the present moment.

"Do not associate happiness with future events. I will be happy when things happen this way. It is like postponing your happiness to an unsure future. The better alternative is to try to postpone your sorrow to some future moment as much as you can. The time to be happy is today because yesterday has already passed, and you cannot be sure that tomorrow will bring any happiness."

"How simple it is to see that we can only be happy now, and there will never be a time when it is not now."

Gerald Jampolsky

Change your thoughts by being a master of your moods.

"Be a master rather than a servant of your own moods. You are the ruler of the kingdom of happiness. Do not allow other people or circumstances to make you happy or sad. Do not depend on material possessions to create happiness for you. It is for you to choose to be happy whatever the situation. Do not allow your heart to break up if your loved one has ditched you. If he/she can be happy without you, so can you."

Wake up with a resolve to stay happy during the day.

"Resolve the first thing as you wake up in the morning to remain happy throughout the day. Spend some time with the flowers and plants in your garden. Listen to the songs of the birds in the trees or watch them flying high in the skies. Or, go out for a walk in the park nearby. Remember your resolve to remain calm as soon as you sense trouble coming. You owe yourself an ethical duty to remain happy."

When you learn to control all your emotions versus allowing them to dictate your mood and actions, you will see the complete transformation in your life. Remember, your emotions, will, and mind are all interlinked, as they are the three components of your soul. Having a well-functioning soul is necessary to shift your narrative from its current storyline to one you design. After reading the last three chapters, changes should have been made, and you should see a new "you" on the horizon.

PART III

Your Future

CHAPTER SIX

Your New Narrative

CHAPTER SIX
THE NEW NARRATIVE

"...and calleth those things which be not as though they were."

Romans 4:17d (BRG)

At the beginning of Chapter Two, I shared this quote: *"Man is nothing else but what he purposes; <u>he exists only in so far as he realizes himself</u>; he is therefore nothing else but the sum of his actions, nothing else but what his life is"* by Jean-Paul Sartre. Take a moment to slowly re-read the underlined portion. Sartre is telling us that we are limited by our vision of ourselves, which ultimately has been shaped by our experiences, our thoughts, our actions, our emotions, and what has entered into our eye and ear gates. Unless we see ourselves as more than what we currently are, we will never progress from our current position. That has been the focus of this entire book- knowing who you are, how you were formed into your current condition, and then working to transform yourself into a version of yourself of which you can be proud.

In this final chapter of the book, let's see where you stand with your transformation and continue building as you strive to progress forward. As you think about where you are, you will likely find that you fit into one of four groups of people who will read this book.

Group One consists of those who have not yet begun the transformation process because they decided to read straight through the book without pausing to put the work in. That is okay because they have already determined they will go back and work their way through the necessary steps. My advice for those in this group is to re-read each chapter (three thru five) for guidance as you transform that part of your life.

Group Two consists of those who have begun working through some of the steps but have not completed the entire process. To ensure your transformation is complete, be sure to dedicate more time to finishing the process. You will be pleased with the outcome when you do.

Group Three consists of those who attended to all the necessary changes and have revealed the "new" person they are. Congratulations to you! I pray you are happy with the results. Also, please note- at any time you see some of the old habits rearing their ugly heads, you can revisit any of the processes to eradicate the behaviors again.

Group Four consists of those who have said they do not see any changes they need to make or are unwilling to make changes for any number of reasons. We all want to see ourselves in a positive light. However, it is best to see ourselves honestly. We cannot prevent others from harming us physically, psychologically, emotionally, or verbally. But, we can prevent ourselves from causing further harm to ourselves by changing harmful practices. So, if you fall into Group Four, rethink your choice about transforming your life.

It is my prayer that all of you at some point will fit into Group Three. We all have something we can change/transform about ourselves. To do so, we must be willing to turn the floodlight onto ourselves to reveal the areas that need improvement.

Remember, transforming yourself does not mean you are a bad or evil person. It just means you understand that to get more out of life and to create a better ending to the narrative you are living, you need to shift some of your perspectives, attitudes, feelings, and/or behaviors. Transforming oneself can be "likened" to the process of metamorphosis.

Metamorphosis, according to dictionary.com, is "a change of the form or nature of a thing or person into a completely different one, by natural or supernatural means." Transformation is likened to metamorphosis in that your form will change but not completely. After your transformation, many of your original characteristics (that make you the unique individual you are) will remain. As I stated at the beginning of the book, you will not undergo a complete overhaul. You will only focus on removing the negative qualities and replacing them with positive ones.

Because all of you will fall into one of the four groups, it is difficult to address you all at once in the different stages you fall in. So, I will address you as though you are all in Group Three, the group that has already completed your personal transformation process, speaking of the transformation as though it is already complete.

The information in this chapter should serve as pointers to keep you focused on being positive and solidifying the shift you have made. To begin, I encourage you to take a deep breath and congratulate yourself for making it this far in your journey of shifting your narrative. With your renewed mindset, take a positive look at all the possibilities and opportunities of the future and begin to call forth those things that were not present before (Romans 4:17d, KJV).

To assist in bringing things to pass in your life, use the power God has provided unto you. Proverbs 18:21 tells us that life and death are in the power of our tongue. So, watch your confession. Be careful what you allow to exit from your lips. Speak positively about your future. At the same time, be honest about what is occurring in your life.

"It is unwise to refuse to face reality; however, if our reality is negative, we can still have a positive attitude toward it. Always be ready mentally to face whatever comes, believing God works good out of everything" (Meyer, 2011, p. 42). Admit your mistakes and when you are wrong. Face reality, but do not allow those mistakes to immobilize you.

While keeping your mind alert and staying positive, watch your confession (the words you speak about yourself and your life). Only speak life into your situation. Positive words and a positive mindset will bring about positive changes in your life.

"For the Scriptures say, 'If you want to enjoy life and see many happy days, keep your tongue from speaking evil and your lips from telling lies.'"

I Peter 3:10 (NLT)

Additionally, we must be cognizant of the thoughts we filter through our mind. Pastor Meyer

(2011) advises, "Thinking about what you're thinking about is very valuable because Satan usually deceives people to into thinking that the source of their misery or trouble is something other than what it really is. He wants them to think they are unhappy due to what is going on around them (their circumstances), but the misery is actually due to what is going on inside of them (their thoughts)" (p. 61).

Also, regardless of the trials that you will face, focus on keeping your mind at peace. A stable mind will lead to positive thoughts and productive actions. "The mind should be kept peaceful. ...when the mind is stayed on the right things, it will be at rest. Yet, the mind should also be alert. This becomes impossible when it is loaded down with things it was never intended to carry" (Meyer, 2011, p. 74).

With your new transformation and a positive mindset, you can now work on fulfilling dreams and visions you may have had but allowed the negative thoughts you held in your mind to stop you from moving forward. Every person has dreams and visions in his/her heart. The dreams begin as little seeds that germinate when they are watered. Like a pregnant woman who nurtures her unborn child while he/she is still in the womb, we nurture our dreams until they come to fruition. However, if prior to the "birth" of the dreams, doubt and fear creep in, we may end up aborting the dreams. Fear and doubt work against our minds to defeat us and extinguish any chance of us being successful. To overcome fear and doubt, take sufficient measures to feel secure about bringing your dreams to fruition, such as writing a business plan, obtaining funding, etc.

Fear and doubt are storms that come to dissuade you from moving forward from fear of failure. The initial cause for fear and doubt to arise could be naysayers who come to rain on your parade by telling you all the pitfalls you may run into or by bringing up failed ventures you have had in the past or the mistakes you may have made. Do not allow the storms to weaken your resolve. Remain steadfast and unmovable! You can succeed! You will be victorious!

"Looking at the past must only be a means of understanding more clearly what and who they are so that they can more wisely build the future."

Paulo Freire
Pedagogy of the Oppressed

We all make mistakes, have struggles, and even regret things in our past. But you are not your mistakes, you are not your struggles, and you are here NOW with the power to shape your day and your future.

Dr. Steve Maraboli

When you examined your past as you read the *Your Current Narrative* chapter, you may have recounted some miserable moments and some regrets. Today, you may even be faced with circumstances you find less than optimal. Circumstances like these and memories of your past can rob you of living a fruitful life today. What will propel you forward is making declarations like the following:

- My future is not determined by my past!
- I am an overcomer!
- I will be victorious!
- I can do this!
- I will not fail!

Our past and the mistakes that occurred are not meant to define us. They are meant to teach us valuable lessons to shape who we will become in our future. We are only the sum total of our mistakes if we continue to make them or focus on them, giving them power over us. If, instead, we learn from them and change for the better by letting go of bad habits and not allowing our past to consume us, our future will be brighter. The choice rests in our hands. Let go of excuses, and take control of your life by leaving the past in the past and seizing the opportunity of today!

When you were a child, you heard many words from your parents, teachers, family members, friends, and even strangers. Those words helped to shape the person you became by either helping to build a strong moral character and mental fortitude within you or causing low self-esteem to develop and/or reckless behavior to manifest. As an adult, you are the main person to speak into your life. Therefore, you must be careful what you say because your ears are ever present, internalizing it all.

As a reminder, Apostle Paul in Philippians 3:13-14 (KJV) tells us, *"Brethren, I count not myself to have apprehended: but this one thing I do, forgetting those things which are behind, and reaching forth unto those things which are before, I press toward the mark for the prize of the high calling of God in Christ Jesus."* This verse tells us to not allow the circumstances, choices, and occurrences of yesterday to sit too heavily on our minds that we cannot focus on moving forward. The past has a way of creeping into our memory and debilitating our progress. That is a trick of the devil. Control the thoughts of your mind and decide what you will focus on and give attention. Keep your mind free from regrets about things you cannot change. Stay focused on creating a brighter today and a more prosperous future.

Furthermore, remember, life and death are in the power of the tongue; speak life (Proverbs

18:21). And, speak those things that be not as though they were (Romans 4:17). When you speak about yourself or about plans you have, be positive, loving, and kind. Refrain from speaking negatively about yourself, and do not allow others to speak negatively about you or your life either. Remain positive and vigilant.

Read this story from Proverbs 6:6-11 (AMPC) as a source of encouragement as you consider moving forward toward your goals.

> ***"Go to the ant, you sluggard; consider her ways and be wise! Which, having no chief, overseer, or ruler, Provides her food in the summer and gathers her supplies in the harvest. How long will you sleep, O sluggard? When will you arise out of your sleep? Yet a little sleep, a little slumber, a little folding of the hands to lie down and sleep. So will your poverty come like a robber or one who travels [with slowly but surely approaching steps] and your want like an armed man [making you helpless]."***

Like the ant, you do not need anyone to motivate you to get a task done or to work toward your dreams. Those who require others to push them will never achieve anything noteworthy. To achieve greatness or to reach a goal, the motivation must begin within and permeate outward.

As you continue to evolve, become someone who is not afraid to take responsibility for your own life. Yes, you will meet resistance. Yes, you will experience challenges and struggles. Through it all, you will build a strong resolve. "Wanting something is not enough – we must also be fully prepared to take responsibility for it" (Meyer, 2011, p. 196).

"All the world's a stage..."
William Shakespeare (1598)

In Chapter Two, I stated our narrative is the story of our life. It is a play (if you will) that is comprised of different acts (seasons), and within each act is a set of scenes that are comprised of days. Each day is a new opportunity for a new adventure in this thing called life. Take advantage of each opportunity to add revelation to your story. Make sure each day, each scene, each act makes an impact and adds substance to your story. Afterall, someone is reading and/or watching the story of your life right now.

What environment are you surrounded by at this very moment? Where do you exist from day to day? Is your environment conducive to promoting the growth and development you desire for yourself? Is your present mindset regarding your abilities limiting your potential? Does your present income level, education level, or health status debilitate your personal growth? While all of these circumstances that encircle you each day may seem to be barriers to the success you desire, the only true barrier is the one you place in your own path. You and you alone can determine your future goals and aspirations. Do not let the current deficiencies of your present circumstances prevent you from bringing your dreams to fruition. You control the narrative!

You are in control of your life and the choices you make, whether right or wrong, wise or foolish, healthy or unhealthy, good or bad. Whatever decision you make, be willing to deal with the consequences of your actions. If you make a decision that did not pan out the way you anticipated, do not let it get you down and do not allow others to put you down. Rise above the choice and move forward. Life is a learning process. Be dedicated to learning and growing on your own terms. People are not required to agree with you or like your choices. Do not live to please others. You are the only one who has to live with you every minute of every day. After all decisions have been made, make sure you can live with yourself.

How you turn out in life is a direct result of where you place your values. Your values result from what you engage in on a regular basis (habitually) because those are the things that are important to you. Specific behaviors/actions are what led to those regular and ongoing patterns in your life. The actions are a direct result of the words you allowed to slip out your mouth. Before the words were formed, you first had a thought. Proverbs 23:7a states, *"For as he thinketh in his heart, so is he."* Everything begins with a thought, whether the thought came quickly and you quickly reacted or whether the thought came and you pondered about it over much time. Either way, a thought came, an action followed, a habit was formed, the habit transformed into a value, and the value played out in your life. Bottom line- control the thoughts of your mind.

Now that you have transformed your thought patterns, emotions, and behaviors, it is time to set goals: short term and long term. Setting and achieving goals should be part of your new narrative. (Note- The next two sections were adapted from *Embracing Womanhood: The Journey of a Queen*, White-Elliott, 2017).

Setting Achievable Goals

Determine your life goals. Ask yourself some important questions about what you want for your life. What do you want to achieve: today, in a year, in your lifetime? The answers to this question can be as general as "I want to be happy," or "I want to help people." Consider what you hope to attain 10, 15, or 20 years from now.

- A career life goal might be to open your own business. A fitness goal might be to become fit. A personal goal might be to have a family one day. These goals can be incredibly broad.

Break the big picture down into smaller and more specific goals. Consider areas of your life that you either want to change or that you would like to develop with time. Areas might include career, finances, family, education, or health. Begin to ask yourself questions about what you would like to achieve in each area and how you would like to approach it within a five-year time frame.

- For the life goal "I want to be fit," you might make the smaller goals "I want to eat more healthily" and "I want to run a marathon."

- For the life goal "I want to open my own business," the smaller goals may be "I want to learn to manage a business effectively," and "I want to open an independent bookstore."

Write goals for the short term. Now that you know roughly what you want to accomplish within a few years, make concrete goals to begin working on now. Give yourself a deadline within a reasonable time frame (no more than a year for short-term goals).

- Writing your goals will make them harder to ignore, consequently making you accountable for them.
- To become fit, your first goals may be to eat more vegetables and to run a 5k.
- To open your own business, your first goals may be to take a bookkeeping class and to find the perfect location for your bookstore.

Make your goals smaller steps that move you towards larger life goals. Basically, you need to decide why you are setting this goal for yourself and what it will accomplish. Some good questions to ask yourself when figuring this out are: Does it seem worthwhile? Is now the right time? Does this match my needs?

- For example, while a short-term fitness goal might be to take up a new sport within six months, ask yourself if that will help you reach your bigger goal of running a marathon. If not, consider changing the short-term goal to something that will be a step towards meeting the life goal.

Adjust your goals periodically. You may find yourself set in your ways concerning broad life goals, but take the time to re-evaluate your smaller goals. Are you accomplishing them according to your time frame? Are they still necessary to keep you on track towards your larger life goals? Allow yourself the flexibility to adjust your goals.

- To become fit, you may have mastered running 5K races. Perhaps after you have run a few and worked on improving your personal best times, you should adjust your goal from "run a 5K" to "run a 10K." Eventually, you can move to "run a half marathon," then "run a marathon."
- To open your own business, after completing the first goals of taking a book-

keeping class and finding a location, you may set new goals to obtain a business loan to purchase a space and to apply for the proper business licensing through your local government. Afterward, you can move towards buying (or leasing) the space, then obtaining the books you need, hiring staff, and opening your doors to business. Eventually, you may even work towards opening a second location!

Practicing Effective Goal Strategies

Make your goals specific. When setting goals, they should answer the highly specific questions of who, what, where, when, and why. For each specific goal you make, you should ask yourself why it is a goal and how it helps your life goals.

- To become fit (which is very general), you have created the more specific goal "run a marathon," which begins with the short-term goal "run a 5K." When you set each short-term goal, such as running a 5K, you can answer the questions: Who? Me. What? Run a 5K. Where? At a local park. When? In six weeks. Why? To work towards my goal of running a marathon.

- To open your own business, you have created the short-term goal "take a bookkeeping class." This can answer the questions: Who? Me. What? Take a book-keeping class. Where? At the Library. When? Every Saturday for five weeks. Why? To learn how to manage a budget for my business.

Create measurable goals. In order for us to track our progress, goals should be quantifiable. "I am going to walk more" is far more difficult to track and measure than "Every day I'm going to walk around the track sixteen times." Essentially, you will need a few ways of determining if you are reaching your goal.

- "Run a 5K" is a measurable goal. You know for certain when you have done it. You may need to set the even shorter-term goal of "run at least three miles, three times every week" to work towards your first 5K. After your first 5K, a measurable goal would be "run another 5K in one month, but take four minutes off of my time."

- Likewise, "take a bookkeeping class" is measurable because it is a specific class that you will sign up to take and go to every week. A less measurable version would be "learn about bookkeeping," which is vague because it is difficult to know when you are "finished" learning about bookkeeping.

Be realistic with your goals. It is important to evaluate your situation honestly and recognize which goals are realistic and which are a little far-fetched. Ask yourself if you have all the things you need to complete your goal (skill, resources, time, knowledge).

- To become fit and run a marathon, you will need to spend a lot of time running. If you do not have the time or interest to devote many hours every week to running, this goal may not work for you. If you find this is the case, you could adjust your goals; there are other ways to become fit that do not involve spending hours and hours running.
- If you want to open your own independent bookstore but you have no experience running a business, have no capital (money) to put towards opening the

business, and you have no knowledge about how bookstores work, or you are not really interested in reading, you may not be successful in achieving your goals.

Set priorities. At any given moment, you may have a number of goals all in different states of completion. Deciding which goals are more important or time-sensitive than others is crucial. If you find yourself with too many goals, you are going to feel overwhelmed and are less likely to accomplish them.

- It may help to choose a few top priorities. This will provide you focus when conflicting goals come up. If it is a choice between completing one or two minor goals and completing one top priority, you know to choose the top priority.
- If you are working towards becoming fit and you have set the smaller goals "to eat more healthily," "to run a 5K," and "to swim one mile, three days per week," you may find that you do not have the time or energy to do all of those things at once. You can prioritize. If you want to run a marathon, first running a 5K may be more important to your goal than swimming every week. You may want to

continue eating better, because that is good for your overall health in addition to helping you run.

- If you are working towards opening your own bookstore, you may need to obtain a business license and be sure you can qualify for a business loan (if you need one) before you begin selecting specific books to carry in your store.

Keep track of your progress. Writing in a journal is a great way to keep track of both personal and professional progress. Checking in with yourself and acknowledging the progress made towards a certain goal is key to staying motivated. It may even encourage you to work harder.

- Asking a friend to keep you on track can help you stay focused. For example, if you are training for the big race, having a friend to regularly meet up with and work out with can keep you on track with your progress.
- If you are getting fit by working towards a marathon, keep a running journal in which you record how far you ran, how much time it took, and how you felt. As you improve more and more, it can be a great confidence boost to go back and

see how far you have come since you started.

- It may be a bit more difficult to track your progress towards opening your own business, but writing down all of your goals and sub-goals, then crossing them out or indicating when each one is complete can help you track the work that you have done.

Assess your goals. Acknowledge when you have reached goals and allow yourself to celebrate accordingly. Take this time to assess the goal process—from inception to completion. Consider if you were happy with the time frame, your skill set, or if the goal was reasonable.

- For example, once you have run your first 5K, be grateful that you have completed a goal, even if it seems small in comparison to your bigger goal of running a marathon.
- Of course, when you open the doors of your independent bookstore and you make your first sale to a customer, you will celebrate, knowing you have worked towards your goal successfully!

Keep setting goals. Once you have achieved goals—even major life goals—you will want to continue to grow and set new goals for yourself.

- Once you run your marathon, you should assess what you would like to do next. Do you want to run another marathon, but improve your time? Do you want to diversify and try a triathlon or an Ironman race? Or, do you want to go back to running shorter distance races—5Ks or 10Ks?
- If you have opened your independent bookstore, do you want to work on implementing community events, such as book clubs or literacy tutoring? Or, do you want to make more money? Would you like to open additional locations or expand by adding a coffee shop inside or next door to your bookstore?

The purpose of setting goals, whether short-term or long-term, is to put your new narrative into action by using all the transformed elements of your soul: your mind, your emotions, and your will. Today is the day to plan for new outcomes as the scenes of your life continue to play out.

As the main character in the story of your life, you have full control over what happens in your life as it relates to your thoughts, your actions, and your emotions. As you control how you feel, what you think, and what you do, plan each day, each year of your life, so that you can be pleased by the results you achieve. Enjoy the new you and walk with your head uplifted being someone you are proud to be, and most of all, love yourself!

Love, love, love yourself!

References

Akin, Imani & Leondra Radford. (2018). "Exploring The Development of Student Self-Esteem and Resilience in Urban Schools" *Contemporary Issues in Education Research (11)*, 1.

American Academy of Family Physicians. 2020. "Mental Health: Keeping Your Emotional Health." familydoctor.org.

Angley, Earnest. (1999). "Live by Faith in the Spiritual Senses" Earnest Angley Ministries. www.ernestangley.org.

Ask the Scientists. (2022). "Making Sense of Your Five Senses" www.askthescientists.com

Barnes, Albert. *Barnes' Notes on the Whole Bible.*

Benson, Joseph. *Commentary of the Old and New Testaments.*

Berg, Yehuda. (2011). huffpost.com.

Bibles for America. (2022). biblesforamerica.org

Brain & Behavior Research Foundation. (2022). "Self-Love and What it Means."

Brenner, Abigail M.D., (2013). "How to Change Your Behavior for Good." *Psychology Today.* Sussex Publishers, LLC.

Eatough, Erin, PhD. (2021). The 6 stages of behavior change: a how-to guide. Betterup.com

Ellicott, Charles John. (1979). *Ellicott's Commentary for English Readers.* Zondervan Publishing.

Faith and Health Connection. (2022) faithandhealthconnection.com

5 Spiritual Senses- G1 Fourways. www.g1fourways.co.za G1Fourways. GodFirstFourways.com

Garrett, Michelle. (2022). 8 Action Steps to Stop Negative Behaviors. www.divaswithapurpose.com.

Gill, John. (1748-63). Gill's Exposition of the Entire Bible. biblehub.com.

GoGuardian Team. (2019). Self-Esteem in Elementary, Middle School, and High School Students. www.goguradianteam.com.

The Gottman Institute. (2022).

Harris, M. A., & U. Orth. (2019). The Link Between Self-Esteem and Social Relationships: A Meta-Analysis of Longitudinal Studies. *Journal of Personality and Social Psychology.*
Harvey & Bradford. (2022). "The Five and More Human Senses." livescience.com
Henry, Matthew. *Matthew Henry's Commentary on the Whole Bible.*
Hongfei, Du, R. B. King, P. Chi. (2012). The development and validation of the Relational Self- Esteem Scale. *Scandinavian Journal of Psychology*. 53(3):258-64.
Kahneman, D. (2000). Evaluation by moments: past and future. In *Choices, values, and frames.* (ed. D. Kahneman and A. Trersky), pp. 293-308. Cambridge University Press and the Russel Sage Foundation, New York.
King, M. (1963). "Letter from Birmingham Jail." *Why We Can't Wait.* (1964). Harper & Row.
King, Martin Luther. 2017. "What is Your Life's Blueprint?" Seattle Times.
Krauss, S. & U. Orth. (2022). Does your work effect your self-esteem and vice versa? www.ejp-blog.com
Locke, John. (1689). *An Essay Concerning Human Understanding.* Oxford University Press.
MacLaren, Alexander. (1959). *MacLaren's Expositions of Holy Scripture.* Eerdmans Publisher.
Merriam-Webster. "Taste." *The Merriam-Webster Dictionary.*
Meyer, J. (2011). Battlefield of the Mind: Winning the battle of your mind. Faith Words, New York.
Nee, Watchman. *Collected Works.* minstrybooks.org
Olds, Tori. (2023). "How Do Experiences Shape Identity?" toriolds.com
Oxford Dictionary. "Liberation."
Poole, Matthew. *A Commentary on the Whole Bible.*
Rishi, Raj. (2023). "15 Powerful Ways to Change Your Thoughts and Transform Your Life" purposefairy.com
Robinson, Lawrence, Jeanne Segal, Ph.D., & Melinda Smith, M.A. (2021). "The Mental Health Benefits of Exercise." helpguide.org.

Sartre, Jean Paul. Goodread quotes.
Sherwood, Chris. (2017). The Effects of Teasing on Children. Healthfully.com
Simply Psychology. (2021). www.simplypsychology.org.
"Tabula rasa." (2022). Britannica.com
"Thoughts, Feelings, and Behaviors." 2021. bridgethegapservices.com.
White-Elliott, C. PhD. (2022). *Pearls of Wisdom.* CLF Publishing, LLC: Hesperia, California.
White-Elliott, C. PhD. (2017). *Embracing Womanhood: The Journey of a Queen*. CLF Publishing, LLC: Hesperia, California.
Wiersbe, Warren. (2007). The Wiersbe Bible Commentary: New Testament. Published by David Cook.

About the Author

Dr. Cassundra White-Elliott resides in California with her family, where as an English/ Education professor, she teaches at various community colleges.

As an author, she composes with the direction of the Holy Spirit, in an effort to share with God's people all He has for them.

In addition to teaching and writing, Dr. Elliott also serves as an evangelistic teacher. She is also the founder of Int'l Women's Commission, a women's ministry that serves the needs of the entire person, by attending to healing the mind, body, soul, and spirit. Her desire is to empower women everywhere.

Dr. Elliott holds a Ph.D. in Education, a Master's degree in English Composition, and a Bachelor's degree in Education.

Dr. Elliott is the founder and editor-in-chief for *Christian Inspiration* magazine, which covers topics germane to Christian living and the world at large.

Dr. Elliott is also the founder of CLF Publishing, LLC. For your publishing needs, go online to www.clfpublishing.org.

Gift of Salvation for Non-Believers

"For all have sinned, and come
short of the glory of God."
(Romans 3:23)

This section was written especially for non-believers, those who have not accepted the gift of salvation. The gift of salvation saves souls from eternal damnation and is a free gift offered by God Himself.

John 3:16-18 says, *"For God so loved the world, that he gave his only begotten Son, that whosoever believeth in him should not perish, but have everlasting life. For God sent not his Son into the world to condemn the world; but that the world through him might be saved. He that believeth on him is not condemned: but he that believeth not is condemned already, because he hath not believed in the name of the only begotten Son of God."*

This section of scripture tells us God's purpose for giving His son Jesus to the world. The world was in a bad condition. The world was over-wrought with sin; the people were living for fleshly desires rather than for God's desires.

As a result of the world's conditions, God decided He would offer the perfect sacrifice that would save the world from being a place where people were lost and had no hope. He decided His own son could stand in proxy for the sin-filled world, taking all sin upon Himself.

So Jesus came, born of a virgin, to save this dying world. He walked on this earth for 33 ½ years, doing the work of His Heavenly Father. At the appointed time, He died by way of crucifixion upon a cross at Calvary, on Golgotha's hill. He shed His blood and died for you and for me. Because His blood was pure, it paid the penalty for all unrighteousness and gave those who believe in Him direct access to His father's throne.

Scripture tells us in Matthew 27:51 that the veil of the temple was ripped in two from top to bottom, at the moment that Jesus' spirit left His body. As a result of the veil's removal, we are no longer required to have a high priest make intercession for us. We, as the children of the Most High God, are able to approach the throne of God for ourselves, and Jesus sits on the right hand of the Father making intercession for us.

But what is even more miraculous than God offering His own son as the perfect sacrifice was the fact that when Jesus was placed in grave clothes and placed in a tomb, He only remained there until the third day. God would not have it that His son would remain in the heart of the earth forever. In order for people to believe in the awesome power of God and His dear son Jesus, a miracle had to be performed. So, on the third day, after Jesus died on the cross, He was resurrected, demonstrating the omnipotence of God. This very act was the act that would cause people to believe in a god that reigns supreme and holds the power of the universe in His very hands, a god that could save them from themselves.

Today, if you are an unbeliever, you can change your destiny. You can change where you will spend your eternity. Our Heavenly Father gives us the freedom of choice about how we want to live our life here on earth and how we want to spend eternity. In Deuteronomy 30:19, God boldly declares, *"I call heaven and earth to record this day against you, that I have set before you life and death, blessing and cursing: therefore choose life, that both thou and thy seed may live."*

So, dear friend what choice will you make today? Will you spend your eternity with the Creator or will you suffer Hell's eternal flames? Again, the choice is yours. Just as the men aboard the ship who were with Jonah became believers, you too can make a choice to accept the only one and true living God as your god.

If after reading the above passages, you have decided that you want to spend your eternity in Heaven with God, the Creator, and His son Jesus, and the Holy Spirit, read through what has affectionately come to be known as the Roman's Road. This is the road to salvation. As you read through the scrip-tures that comprise the Roman's Road, you will also read the explanation for each scripture, so you will have clarity about what you are reading and confessing.

The Roman's Road to Salvation

The road to salvation begins with Romans 3:23 which declares, "*For all have sinned, and come short of the glory of God.*" This scripture explains that everyone has come short of God's glory and needs redemption. Then, Romans 6:23a states, "*For the wages of sin is death.*" Here, we learn that the consequence of living a life of sin is death. Everyone will experience physical death as a result of the sin committed in the garden of Eden, but those who commit themselves to a life of sin will suffer eternal damnation in the lake of fire (Rev. 19). Continue with the rest of verse 6:23 that says, "*but the gift of God is eternal life through Jesus Christ our Lord.*" There is an alternative to suffering eternal damnation. We can accept the gift of salvation by accepting Jesus as our personal Lord and Savior. Then, Romans 5:8 says, "*But God commendeth his love toward us, in that, while we were yet sinners, Christ died for us.*" We are able to receive the gift of salvation because Christ came to earth and shed His blood for us on the cross.

Continue to Romans 10: 9-10 which says, "*That if thou shalt confess with thy mouth the Lord Jesus, and shalt believe in thine heart that God hath raised him from the dead, thou shalt be saved. For with the heart man believeth unto righteousness; and with the mouth confession is made unto salvation.*" If we confess with our mouths that Jesus is the son of God, that He came and died for our sins, and that God raised Him from the dead, we will receive salvation.

Finish with Romans 10:13, which states, "*For whosoever shall call upon the name of the Lord shall be saved.*" Call upon the name of God by saying these words, **"Lord Jesus, come into my heart and save me, Lord. I believe that you are the Son of God who came and died on the cross for my sins. I believe that you rose from the grave. I also believe that you now sit in heaven on the right side of the Father, making intercession for me. I accept you as my Lord and my Savior."**

Now that you have confessed with your mouth that Jesus is the son of God and that He died for our sins and rose from the grave, **YOU ARE NOW SAVED!!!!** You will spend your eternity in heaven.

The next step is very important- you must find a Bible-based church that teaches the Word of God and confesses the Lord Jesus Christ to be the son of God. Don't delay. Do this immediately. Do not leave yourself open to the enemy. Get connected with the saints of the Most High God and keep yourself covered with the unspotted blood of the Lamb.

Here is my prayer for you.

Father God,

I thank you for the opportunity to minister your word to the unsaved, the unchurched, and the uncommitted. Father God, I pray now for the souls who have just received the gift of salvation. Lord Father, they have opened their hearts to you, and I know that you have received them into your kingdom and written their names in the Book of Life. Father God, I pray that you will touch their lives and show yourself mightily before them. Let their eyes be opened by the scales falling off, allowing them to see clearly.

Father God, I even pray for the backslider, those who have turned away from you after receiving the gift of salvation. You said in your Word that you desire that none would perish. So Lord, I send your Word to them right now, praying that they would confess the iniquity in their heart, repent, and turn from their evil ways, so that they may receive a life of abundance. You said in your Word in Matthew Chapter 14, that every knee shall bow before you and every tongue will confess that Jesus is Lord.

Father God, I pray now that we all come under subjection to your Word and that we will humbly submit our lives to you. I ask all these things in the name of my Lord and Savior Jesus Christ.
Amen, Amen, Amen!!!!

I will continue to pray for your success in your walk with God. Remember, this spiritual walk that you are about to embark on will not be an easy walk, but remember, the race is not given to the swift but to those who endure to the end.

Be blessed with heaven's best. I love you!

Additional Titles by the Author

Public Speaking in the Spiritual Arena (2002)
Do You Know God? (2004)
Unleashed Anger, Anger Unleashed (2005)
Unleashed Anger Daily Prayer Guide (2005)
Two of a Kind (2006)
Dare to Succeed by Breaking Through Barriers (2007)
Dare to Succeed Prayer Guide (2007)
Through the Storm (2007)
Lord, Teach Me to be a Blessing! (2007)
The Preacher's Daughter (2007)
The Preacher's Son (2009)
Where is Your Joppa? (2009)
From Despair, through Determination, to Victory! (2009)
Fear Not (2011)
Mayhem in the Hamptons (2012)
After the Dust Settles (2013)
A Mother's Heart (2013)
A Diamond in the Rough (2013)
The Power of a Woman (2013)
365 Days of Encouragement (2013)
A Touch in the Dark (2014)
Broken Chains (2014)
I Have Fallen (2014)
The Bottom Line (2015)
Set Free (2015)
Daughter, God Loves You (2016)
A Mother's Heart II (2016)
Living a Balanced Life (2016)
Kimara and Aaron Go to Disneyland (2016)
Embracing Womanhood (2017)
A Mother's Heart III (2017)
Web of Lies (2017)
Time is Running Out (2017)
Revisiting Grammar & Business Writing Essentials (2017)
Test Preparation: Writing Essentials, Mathematics Review & Reasoning Skills (2017)
The Making of Dr. C. (2018)

Claim Your Inheritance (2018)
Women's Study Bible New International Version (2018)
Christian Inspiration (2019-present)
Safety in Him (2019)
A Mother's Heart IV (2019)
A is for Adam (2019)
Have You Walked in My Shoes? (2019)
Prepare for Battle (2019)
B is for Babel (2020)
C is for Christ (2020)
D is for David (2020)
E is Eve (2020)
F is for Forgiveness (2020)
G is for Givers (2020)
H is for Helping Others (2020)
I is for Idols (2020)
J is for Joseph (2020)
K is for Kindness (2020)
The Last Shall Be First: An Analysis of the Systemic Subdivide of Black America (2021)
L is for Love (2021)
M is for Mary (2021)
N is for Noah's Ark (2021)
is for Obedience (2021)
Rest in Him: Scriptures for Daily Peace (2021)
P is for Paul the Apostle (2021)
Q is for Queen Esther (2021)
Be Ye Inspired Vol. 1 (2021)
R is for Ruth (2021)
Be Ye Inspired Vol. II (2022)
S is for Samuel (2022)
T is for Truth (2022)
U is for Unconditional Love (2022)
V is for Victory (2022)
W is for Worship (2022)
X is for Xerxes the Persian King (2022)
Y is for You (2022)
Pearls of Wisdom (2022)
Z is for Zachariah (2022)
Pearls of Wisdom Quotes & Journal (2022)

www.ingramcontent.com/pod-product-compliance
Lightning Source LLC
Chambersburg PA
CBHW040224110426
42813CB00048B/3449/J

* 9 7 8 1 9 4 5 1 0 2 9 3 6 *